Masters of the Poster 1896-1900

Reproduces the complete text
and all the plates in the series
"Les Maîtres de l'Affiche."

256 color plates

———

Preface by Roger Marx

Introduction by Alain Weill

Notes by Jack Rennert

———

Images Graphiques, Inc./New York

The prints from *Maîtres de l'Affiche* reproduced in this volume were all photographed from the collection of Park South Gallery at Carnegie Hall, New York City. To its director, Ms. Laura Gold, who has done so much to popularize the original poster and the *Maîtres* series, our special thanks for allowing us to reproduce these plates from her collection.

Translated by Bernard Jacobson.

© Copyright 1977 Images Graphiques, Inc.

IMAGES GRAPHIQUES, INC.
37 Riverside Drive
New York, New York

Library of Congress Catalog Card Number: 77-94468

ISBN (Softcover) 0-89545-013-5
ISBN (Hardcover) 0-89545-012-7

All rights reserved, which includes the right to reprint this book or portions thereof in any form whatsoever.

Printing Printing, November 1977.

Printed in the United States of America.

Introduction

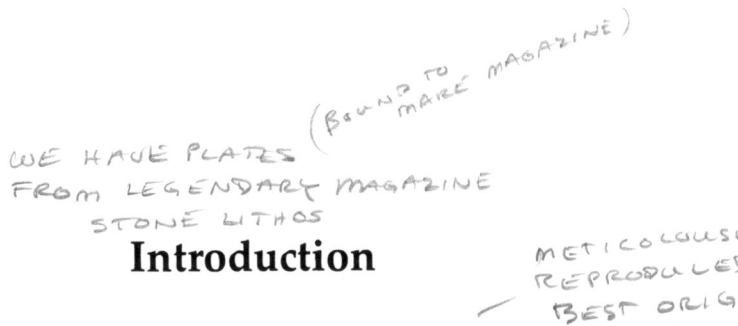

The publication of *Les Maîtres de l'Affiche* from 1895 to 1900 appears to have been the logical consequence of the vogue of this new artistic means of expression, the poster, which had just been invented by Jules Chéret in the 1860's. The popularity of the poster spread quickly from France to other parts of the world during the last twenty years of the 19th Century. Transgressing their initial advertising function, posters became art objects, much sought after by collectors. Henri Beraldi wrote in 1886: "Now it is the poster that brings enjoyment to the print collector." (*Les Graveurs au XIXe siècle*. Conquet Editeur, 1886.)

Posters could be found in special galleries such as Sagot's (who was the first to offer a catalogue in 1891), Arnould's or Pierrefort's. *La Plume*, a magazine which, starting in November 1893 (Issue #110, "The Illustrated Poster") regularly devoted special editions to the subject, also sold posters by mail. Though the first exhibit of posters dates back to 1884, at the Théâtre de la Galerie Vivienne, in Paris, many more were organized during the last decade of the century: in France, at Nantes (1889), Nancy (1890), Paris (International Advertising Exhibit of 1891, Exhibit organized by Sagot at the Bodinière in 1892, also in 1895), in Rouen (1895), Toulouse (Belgian Poster Exhibition, 1896), Avesnes (1896), Reims (1896) and the Paris World's Fair (1900), to name only the most important ones. Outside of France, similar events were taking place: Five poster exhibitions in Great Britain, the first one in 1894-95 at the Royal Aquarium in London, six in the United States, beginning with one at the Pratt Institute in Brooklyn, others in Belgium, one in Germany (Dresden, 1896) and in Italy (Milan, 1894).

The proliferation of posters and the public's love for the medium induced critics and editors to publish, from 1895 on, numerous magazines, reference works and documentation on the subject. In France, the most important periodicals were, in addition to the special editions of *La Plume* and *La Critique*, *L'Estampe et l'Affiche* (1897-1899) and *L'Image* (1896-1897). In the United States, in addition to articles on the subject in *Scribner's* Magazine, there appeared such short-lived magazines as *The Bill Poster* and *Poster Lore*. In England articles were published in *The Studio* and *The Poster Magazine*. In Belgium articles on the subject were printed in *L'Affiche artistique*. In Paris, Ernest Maindron wrote the important *Les Affiches illustrées* (1896), Emile Bauwens published *Les Affiches etrangères* (1897) and Demeure de Beaumont brought out *L'Affiche Belge* (1897). In New York's bookstores there appeared a collection of the *Scribner* articles, *The Modern Poster*, and, in 1896, *Posters in Miniature*, a work that is analogous to *Les Maîtres de l'Affiche*. And in New York's leading bookstore, Brentano's, many of the original posters reproduced in this volume were being sold for about $3.00 to $5.00. In London, in 1895, Charles Hiatt published *The Illustrated Poster*.

This quick enumeration demonstrates how, in a limited timespan, many works on the poster appeared on the market. It is in this context that we must place *Les Maîtres de l'Affiche*.

At the time posters posed a problem which, moreover, has still not been solved: how to keep and enjoy a collection consisting of very large size prints which one has to preserve rolled or flat in some cabinet. It is probably one of the reasons why *Les Maîtres de l'Affiche* was published. The book provided a reduction of the most valued and consequently the most widely known posters, thus enabling collectors and other interested people to examine quickly and easily the main works of the current advertising production. Moreover, the content of these five volumes is without great surprises. Chéret was the artistic director of the publisher, the Imprimerie Chaix. In 1890, the French Government bestowed upon him its greatest honor, making him a "Chevalier de la Légion d'Honneur," for, since 1866, he had created virtually a new industry, the application of art to commercial and industrial printing. He was the embodiment of the poster's triumph and *Les Maîtres de l'Affiche* was something of a tribute to the master. At the time he was 60 years old and the major part of his work had been accomplished. In fact, he practically ceased to produce advertising works from this time, devoting himself mostly to painting and by 1900 he definitely opted for this medium entirely.

One out of four posters, the first of each monthly installment, is by Chéret. This gives us a total of 60 (some of these appeared in the book before they reached the market place) without counting the bonus prints (here referred to as "Special Plates"). Half of the remaining works reproduced here are signed by French artists and they are a collection of posters which the critics and the dealers considered "artistic." This excludes, by definition, many anonymous posters which were often of great quality such as works by Appel or Lévy and the works of graphic artists who had not, or had not yet, made a name for themselves. In this volume we find Lautrec and Bonnard side by side with Mucha and Grasset as well as Guillaume and Pal. The last fourth of the collection is dedicated to foreign posters. If we evaluate the content of exhibits and books devoted to the period, in France as well as abroad, we must come to the conclusion that this proportion is just a reflection of French preponderance in the medium and, for once, this should not be seen as excessive chauvinism. We do come across the most important English, Belgian and American posterists. The minimal representation of Germany, Austria, Italy and Russia is due to the fact that in these countries the poster came of age only later.

The economics of this volume, as well as of the originals of the posters it reproduced, are most interesting to contemplate today. *Les Maîtres de l'Affiche* sold in Paris for 2.50 francs for four issues (one month's subscription) and for 27 francs for 12 monthly offerings, or 48 reproductions (plus the bonus plates). To get an idea of what these sums mean, let's turn to the classified advertising of the period: to get into the "Moulin de la Galette" dance hall cost you 1.50 francs, to the Folies-Bergère, 2.00 francs; dinner at the Taverne de l'Ermitage on the Boulevard de Clichy was 3.00 francs. A tourist class round trip train ticket Paris-Dieppe, Dieppe-Paris cost 6.00 francs. A yearly subscription to the illustrated humor weekly *Le Rire* was 8.00 francs. At the Belle Jardiniere, vested suits were available for 28.00 francs and overcoats for 22.00 francs. A simple 13×18 camera could be purchased for 135.00 francs. These few prices show that a substantial part of the urban population could afford to buy *Les Maîtres de l'Affiche*, a fact that was confirmed by the bookstores' advance orders.

A comparison of the price of *Les Maîtres de l'Affiche* with the price of original works is also very interesting and maybe surprising. In the catalogues, almost all the posters created by artists, from Lautrec to Guillaume, including Bonnard, Steinlen, Mucha, deFeure and the leading foreign posterists, sold for 2.50 to 5.00 francs each (with a maximum price of 25.00 francs for Lautrec's "La Goulue" at the Moulin

Rouge, in large format and mounted on cloth), that is to say the same as one or two month's issues (four or eight reproductions) of *Les Maîtres de l'Affiche*.

Moreover, this is not at all surprising since the posters were printed in great quantities on ordinary paper and, to boot, the one-time art and plate costs were assumed by the company whose product it advertised; the dealers paid printers only for the overrun they wished to acquire. Hence, we must consider it normal that *Les Maîtres de l'Affiche*, specially produced by means of lithography, on quality paper, was offered for sale at the price of an original poster. The people did not perceive these two types of products as being in competition. They were infatuated with small prints and with this kind of compilation. Other publications of this type, for instance *L'Estampe Originale* and *L'Estampe Moderne*, were being offered at the same time. The bonuses offered to the subscribers of *Les Maîtres de l'Affiche* were not posters but rather decorative lithographs; this clearly shows that it was this print-buying public that the publishers had in mind. We do not know how many copies of *Les Maîtres de l'Affiche* had been printed but judging from the number of plates that have been found in France the number must have been high. And yet the demand for original copies remains so high, eighty years later, that individual plates of *Les Maîtres de l'Affiche* sell today for $50.00 to over $500.00.

Presently, after a long eclipse, interest in the poster grows each day. This reprint of the now very rare five volumes of *Les Maîtres de l'Affiche*, an invaluable reference tool, is surely a timely event.

—Alain Weill
Paris, France
September, 1977

ALAIN WEILL is curator of the newly-formed Musée de l'Affiche (The Poster Museum of Paris) which now houses the collection which he previously supervised at the Musée des Arts Décoratifs. He is an acknowledged authority in the field of poster history and, in addition to mounting many exhibitions and writing many articles and catalogues on the subject, he is author of two books, *100 Years of Posters of the Folies-Bergère and Music Halls of Paris* and *Art Nouveau Postcards*. He is presently at work on a book titled *100 Posters of Jules Chéret*.

Acknowledgments

This volume represents the collaborative effort and helping hand of many individuals. We are grateful to all of them, although only a few can be mentioned here.

Photographs were carefully made by Mr. Martin F. Jackson. As always, Mr. Kanae Akiyama of Daiichi Seihan showed great care and concern in the handling of color separations; he was assisted by Mr. Tomeji Maruyama. The design and layout was under the supervision of Mr. Harry Chester, assisted by Mr. Alexander Soma of his staff. Precision Typoraphers did careful composition work. Printing was in the capable hands of Mr. Andrew Merson and Mr. Gary Feller and we are especially indebted to everyone at MacNaughton Lithograph Co. and Command Web Offset Co. And the staff of Images Graphiques helped in countless ways: special thanks are due to Ms. Helen Garfinkle and Mr. Stu Solow.

—The Publisher.

Notes

The historic importance of *Maîtres de l'Affiche* is so widely acknowledged, and its context and background so well summarized by M. Alain Weill in his introduction to this book, and its editor, Roger Marx, so rightfully praised for so much good encouragement given to the poster, that it seems a bit disrespectful and small-minded to more closely examine the validity of the entire series. And yet, this note, directed to collectors and would-be collectors of the poster, is meant to be critical—but, hopefully, in the most constructive sense.

When looking at any collection, whether it be war posters or record album covers or vintage postcards, the process of collection can be as fascinating to the viewer as it is to the collector: The criteria for choice—why was this poster selected, that one excluded? — is an interesting game for the viewer and gives us a revealing portrait, often unintentional, of the collector. I perhaps approach it more personally than most readers, because as someone who avidly collects original posters and publishes, edits and writes books on the subject, I know only too-well the very painful process involved in such selection. And so, for me to look at the selections in *Maîtres de l'Affiche* is invariably to try to second-guess its editor, or, at the very least, to look over his shoulder and try to find the reasoning behind particular choices.

One could spend endless hours—and pages—speculating on why one's favorite poster is not included in this collection: Why isn't a single Aristide Bruant poster of Lautrec reproduced? Why two mundane charity posters by Chéret (89, 161) and not two of his very best, such as the spectacular La Danse du Feu or the elegantly beautiful Librairie Sagot? Why Hazenplug's "Living Posters" but none of his equally beautiful Chap Book works? Such questions in no way detract from a collection or a publication. An editor is allowed his opinion; in fact, we tend to respect the opinionated ones all the more. This is the fun of collecting—in any field.

Maîtres — and France

But there is simply too much of an imbalance in this collection to allow us to go through it without more critical concern. The imbalance is first geographic: Of the 240 posters reproduced here, 179 are French (180 if you include Grasset's poster printed in the United States; Plate 126). While I would be the last to accuse my learned colleague M. Weill of "excessive chauvinism," I simply to do not feel, by the criteria established by both the publisher Chaix and the editor Roger Marx, that it is a fair representation to have such a large portion of French posters.

And what were those criteria? In the advertisement they placed at the end of the second year, reproduced and translated here, Chaix, the publisher, promised reproductions "interesting at once for the quality and the variety of the reproductions." There can be no argument about quality—looking at the original prints 80 years later one still marvels at their technical perfection. But what about "variety"? Chaix went on to declare that, "It seemed to us that all artists of talent, whatever their style, should be represented, the young artists side by side with their seniors, without preference or prejudice." Universality was to be the scope; quality the sole criteria.

And Chaix was merely echoing the sentiments of Roger Marx. In a revealing paragraph of the preface to the first volume, he states: "It fell to the Imprimerie Chaix, where Jules Chéret published so many radiant masterpieces, now considered classics, to take the initiative of this publication, to assure its success by means of a selection free from prejudice and a reproduction which is the perfection of the chromolithographic process. Grouped fraternally, the masters of Europe and America will see their most important pages included in this Pantheon of the modern poster and reflect there, according to temperament, climate, race, the infinite diversity of the human genius." It is in its own quest for "diversity" that it is most lacking; *Maîtres* simply is *not* "free from prejudice." Germans, Austrians (there is not a single Klimt), Italians are simply not given their due in what is purported to be an international showcase. Americans do better, but one finds two Penfields (20, 115) at a time when there were 29 different Penfields exhibited, in 1896, at the Reims Exposition d'Affiche (where almost all the posters in *Maîtres* were exhibited). His two Harper's are fine, but there were many others of equal or higher stature—equal and higher than many French posters.

Maîtres — and Jules Chéret.

A second imbalance has to do with artists represented, most glaringly the overabundant representation of Jules Chéret. Each month's offering began with a Chéret poster. That means 25%, or 60 poster plates out of 240 were by Chéret, and if we add to this the special or bonus plates offered subscribers—we note that 7 of the 16 were by him—we have a total of 67 out of 256 plates. (This is vividly brought out in this volume: The upper left hand corner of each page is a poster by Chéret.) There can be no doubt about the importance of Chéret in the history of the pictorial poster—he founded an art form, a marketing medium and a lithographic industry, almost singlehandedly.

And Chaix knew exactly what they were getting when they asked Roger Marx to write the preface to each year's compendium of reproductions. Roger Marx had a special fondness for the works of Chéret and this can be seen as a natural outgrowth of his life's work. (See our biographical note.) Surely one of the warmest appreciations for Chéret's work was the introduction written by Roger Marx for the "Exposition Jules Chéret" held in 1889 at the

Galeries du Théâtre d'Application in Paris. The catalogue was, of course, printed by Chaix. In it, Roger Marx extolled Chéret's virtues as a creator of the pictorial poster, and, possibly quite inadvertently, but nonetheless revealingly, indicated some of his own philosophy on the subject:

"To wrest the street from the gray and bleak monotony of buildings strung in long rows; to cast upon them the fireworks of color, the glow of joy; to convert the walls into 'decorable' surfaces and let this open air museum reveal the character of a people and at the same time become the subconscious education of the public taste, such is Chéret's task. From the whim of his genius have sprung into view, under the pretext of advertisements, a thousand charming, merry evocations. He raised the poster to the level of the art print; prior to Chéret the poster was dull or of no interest, but then it began to draw from the painter's palette its element of seduction, its chance to succeed, to persuade. Thus, for twenty or more years, Chéret toyed with the arduous themes which the feverish need for advertising submitted to him for illustration, and he seized upon the ever increasing advertising fever to take hold of the big city and to impose upon it an imaginative and ever changing appearance and to become, in fact, the sole decorator of present day Paris."

But the purpose of *Maîtres* was clearly more than praise, however much deserved, for the artistic director of the publisher. And this overemphasis of one artist's work was at the expense of that of others. Even French posterists were slighted: There are no posters at all by Henri Boutet, by Hermann Paul, by Abel Truchet, and too few by many others.

Another imbalance, closely associated with the overemphasis on Chéret, is the predominance of his printing plant: There are 88 posters here which were originally printed by Chaix, 19 by Verneau, and not a single other printer has more than 5!

But it is when we get to such glaring omissions as not a single poster by John Hassall, whose most productive period coincided with the publication years of *Maîtres*; when we see only one poster by Pal, who had over 100 different posters on sale at Sagot, La Plume, Arnould and other dealers and galleries at this very time and 34 posters on display at the Reims exhibition; when one does not see a single poster by Friedlander of Hamburg or Strobridge in the United States; when one sees only two posters printed by the great French lithographer Appel and only one by Charles Lévy—it is when looking at these facts that one sees more than an editor's choice at work, but a whole way of looking at posters which is really at the core of the imbalance of *Maîtres* and, to me, its most serious drawback.

Probably the most popular poster of its time was the show poster—the poster for touring theatrical companies, for the circus, for the café-concert and other popular entertainments—and it is these posters that were most widely seen by people and which *Maîtres* so flagrantly ignored. True, the title is "Maîtres"—masters—but we are led to believe, by editor and publisher, that anonymity of creation and popularity of product need not be opposites, and yet not a single anonymous poster is allowed on these pages. And again we can judge by the very criteria set up by the editor: The poster as "the people's art" is continously stressed by Roger Marx in all his writings and is frequently cited in his prefaces here. The posters are to be judged by people in the street, he tells us, and it's there that "the public's vote is cast."

But, essentially, as M. Weill correctly notes in his introduction, it was the print collector to whom Roger Marx was addressing himself and for whom *Maîtres* was intended. And the print collector is, well, a better and more educated person than you and or I. His aspirations and tastes are more elevated. Summing up his five years' work, Roger Marx returned to the motivation of the publication: "For five years, it was the task of *Les Maîtres de l'Affiche* to reveal the state of mural chromolithography at the end of the century; in addition, by letting the masterpieces emerge from the flood of the current production we have administered a lesson of high eclecticism and established favorable points of reference for the orientation of taste." Again, this ambivalence and contradiction: "the state of mural chromolithography" and "masterpieces" to teach us a "high lesson"; this may be untenable. So many of the very best posters—by the standards of Roger Marx relating to public acceptance, such as the show and popular entertainment posters previously referred to—simply do not qualify for a place of honor because, according to the other standard of excellence, they do not raise our taste. And so, although publication of *Maîtres* coincided also with the golden period of the traveling tent shows and circuses and hundreds of thousands of bright and beautiful posters to advertise their coming flooded the cities and countrysides all over Europe as well as the United States, not a single Barnum and Bailey, or Buffalo Bill poster will be found here; they may have enjoyed great success with the people in the street but they were anonymously created —and print collectors are above all name collectors for whom anonymity is anathema—and, furthermore, such posters appeal to the most basic and elemental of human instincts, desires and fears. The opera may be uplifting, the circus is sheer magic and joy. But print collectors are a serious lot, spending as much time cataloguing and preserving as in looking and appreciating. It is no accident that all the great show printers, from Friedlander in Germany, to Strobridge in the United States, to Lévy and Appel in Paris, were thus entirely ignored or slighted by *Maîtres*. (If Lévy's sole poster in *Maîtres* had not been by Lautrec, he would also have been completely shut out.)

It is because of the very high esteem of *Maîtres*, not only during its period of publication, but in the ensuing years—with posters reproduced in it being far more valued than those omitted, and far more frequently discussed in books and journals—that this orientation is all the more regrettable. It did, in fact, represent the collecting tastes of its time, and its failure, if it can be called that, is that it reflected it rather than corrected it or lead it into the very directions it espoused. And poster histories since that time have echoed this selection; and as print dealers have become poster dealers in the past two decades, this has further grafted a "print-mentality" to what should be a truly popular art form—very possibly the only one deserving of that cliché, "the people's art."

Maîtres—and Roger Marx

One of the mysteries that has never been cleared to my satisfaction is the exact relationship between Roger Marx and the selection of the posters to be reproduced in *Maîtres*. Did he directly chose what was to go in? Or was he merely asked to provide a preface to each year's volume? Possibly, it might have been something in between, with Roger Marx taking an advisory role in the selection process.

One can only speculate. From the evidence at hand, I draw a few personal conclusions: One does not go through thousands of posters, consciously select a few for publication in an important collector's portfolio without telling the reader something in greater detail about that painful process. There is a need to justify inclusions and omissions that can be found in any art book that goes far beyond the generalizations found in Roger Marx's prefaces. Other than tossing a few more bouquets at Chéret, almost no artist is mentioned by name; his statements about the importance of the poster can only be cheered, but they are as mundane as they are true.

Another clue is more explicit: In the Preface to the first volume Roger Marx states that, "It fell to the Imprimerie Chaix . . . to take the initiative of this publication, to assure its success by means of a selection free from prejudice. . . ." This sounds more like a guide showing one a completed building rather than a worker toiling to build it.

Maîtres: Chronology and Size

It is easier to indicate what *Maîtres* is *not*: It is *not* the product of an editor who looked at each month's poster production from all over the world and picked the four he thought best for reproduction in a collection. One of the most obvious things about these posters is that they bear no chronological relation whatsoever: One can quickly see this by looking though the Numerical Table of Reproductions. Even works of the same artist are wildly "out of sequence": One wonders why it was necessary in 1899 (Pl. 165) to dredge up a Chéret poster (1884) executed 15 years earlier! Or why Lautrec's first poster (1891) does not make its appearance until Volume III in 1898, the fourth of his five posters reproduced here! Almost all the posters reproduced here were widely available for sale at the time and all had been shown at one or another of the major exhibitions in the 1890's.

One final point about chronology which ties in with my own feelings that Roger Marx had little to do with the actual compilation of these volumes is the overall sloppiness of the research of the collection. Some of this I allude to in my remarks preceding the Numerical Listings. The fact is that of the 240 posters, 64 were listed without any year of publication. Today, my colleagues and I who write books and catalogues on the subject, toil for hours and days to locate the exact date of publication of a poster; since these posters are often from foreign lands and from a time long ago—many from a previous century—we can be forgiven an occasional error or "circa" notation before a date. But to edit a book of contemporary artists, many of whom one knows intimately, to have that book printed by the firm which produced the majority of such posters in their original format and featured their own artistic director in so many cases—the firm who printed all the color plates in Maindron's *Les Affiches Illustrées*, which was just published as *Maîtres* began and which fully documented all these facts—and then to omit the dates or get them wrong, well, that is plain sloppy. It should be noted that the cover of the monthly installment of four reproductions did not list the dates; the dates appear only in the yearly compendiums and, no doubt, some clerk, assigned the task of placing dates at the end of the yearly bound volumes' index, found it too tedious a job. But there is a question here about the level of personal involvement of Roger Marx: Would he knowingly consent to such errors of omission and such inconsistencies?

The reader should be aware that we have reproduced each plate to the exact proportion of the image area on the print originally produced by Chaix. The size of each print—there were four reproductions each month—was 11-¼ by 15-½ inches (28.5 × 39.5 cm) but the image area changed greatly within that sheet-size. It is this image area that we have reproduced to scale. Why some posters were produced larger than others is another mystery of *Les Maîtres*. For instance, take a look at plates 61 (Chéret's Paris Courses) and 62 (Georges Meunier's Trianon Concert): The size of the original posters was identical, 124 by 88 cm, but plate 61 has an image area which is 33 cm (13 inches) high while plate 62 has an image area which is only 28 cm (11 inches) high and therefore appears to be a smaller poster, both in the original *Maîtres* and in the reproduction in this volume which, again, we have kept to scale. (A paranoic view would see this as further conspiracy to assure that Chéret remained "higher" than others, but the table is often turned: Plate 79, Morrow's poster for "The New Woman," is given a larger reproduction than the Chéret's for Vin Mariani, Plate 77, when in fact Chéret's poster is twice the size of the English one.)

In spite of all these criticisms, one again comes back to *Maîtres*, and one comes back to it time and again, not only as a valuable research tool, but as a sheer pleasure to view. The reader who has never seen these reproductions is advised to visit a local gallery or library; they are precious gems of the finest examples of the lithographer's trade and it is remarkable how well they have stood the test of time. (If one were to select the best posters—by any criteria—of the 1970's and issue their reproduction four times each month for the next five years, would our grandchildren treasure them and hold them in high esteem in the year 2050? That's a difficult question to answer, but it gives a measure of the success of *Maîtres*.) Hopefully this reprint of *Maîtres* will spur people to collect not only these original prints, but the original posters themselves.

Finally, Roger Marx's message is as timeless and relevant as the posters themselves: In 1898, in the preface to Volume IV, he wrote: "More so than any of its predecessors, our generation has become concerned with the esthetics of the street." Concern for our environment is a clarion call everywhere today, and hopefully, this book can make its greatest contribution by removing the POST NO BILLS signs from our streets and stations and public places of all kinds and, through the help of such colorful, beautifully-designed posters, end "the gray and bleak monotony of buildings strung in long rows" and "cast upon them the fireworks of color, the glow of joy."

—Jack Rennert
New York
October 1977

November 1, 1897

The Masters of the Poster

TO OUR SUBSCRIBERS

IMPRIMERIE CHAIX
Rue Bergère, 20
PARIS

The publication of **The Masters of the Poster** is about to begin next month, its third year of existence, and, on this occasion, we would like to take the opportunity to thank our subscribers for the welcome they have given it and for the encouragements they have sent our way.

When we created this collection, we thought it ought to form a gallery, interesting at once for the quality and the variety of the reproductions. It seemed to us that all artists of talent, whatever their style, should be represented, the young artists side by side with their seniors, without preference nor prejudice. It is in this spirit that we have presented until now to our subscribers fifty-seven different artists: thirty Frenchmen and twenty-seven foreigners.

Again, in our third series, the subscriber will find the French masters whose talent he has been able to appreciate in the preceding volumes: Jules Chéret, Grasset, Willette, Lautrec, Ibels, Steinlen, Boutet de Monvel, Mucha, Réalier-Dumas. We plan to add to this list the names of several distinguished designers who have not yet been represented in our publication: Anquetin, Valloton, Grün, Luce, Léopold Stévens, Lucas.

A large section will be devoted to foreign posters which, in the preceding series, have been received with such great success. Among the British, the American, Belgian, German and Czech artist: Beggarstaff, Fred Hyland, Dudley-Hardy, Louis Rhead, Woodbury, Penfield, Miss Ethel Reed, Bradley, Privat-Livemont, Rassenfosse, Berckmans, Evenepoël, Otto Fischer and Oliva will contribute their very personal and expressive compositions.

Finally, to give an advantage to those who subscribe to twelve consecutive issues, we offer them four annual bonuses instead of two, executed by our most renowned artists.

We will be happy if we can, by means of this program, fulfill the wishes of our subscribers.

RENEWAL OF SUBSCRIPTIONS
THIRD SERIES

The twenty-fourth installment (November 1897) of **The Masters of the Poster** *completes the second series.*

Hence, the subscribers are requested to renew their subscriptions **before November 15th.**

Those subscribers who obtained their subscription through a bookdealer should again address their request for renewal to the same dealer.

Price of the 12 issue subscription

		On Japan Paper
Paris	Fr. 27	80
Provinces, Algeria, Tunis	Fr. 28	81
Foreign countries and Colonies (Postal Union)	Fr. 30	83

I declare that I would like to renew my subscription for twelve installments beginning with December 1, 1897, for the sum of _____ which I enclose herewith.

Send this stub to Mr. Alban Chaix, administrative director of the Chaix Printing Co., 20 rue Bergère, Paris—or to the dealer from whom the original subscription was obtained.

Paris, December 15, 1897

BINDINGS FOR THE TWELVE INSTALLMENTS
OF THE SECOND SERIES

We are putting at the disposal of the subscribers and single issue buyers a special binding with an artistic cover which will hold the twelve issues that comprise the second series.

This cover, designed by Mr. Paul Berthon, is printed in five colors, with special metallic inks, on embossed cloth binding.

Subscribers or single issue buyers who wish to obtain it may send their order to us, enclosing a postal money order or cashier's check.

PRICE:

PARIS	Fr. 8
Provinces et Foreign countries (Postal Union)	Fr. 9

ROGER MARX
(1859-1913)

Born in Nancy, France, in 1859, Roger Marx had a brilliant career as an art critic and historian. His interests were eclectic; his mind always inquisitive. His genius was that he never just reflected or commented on the current art scene, but that he saw its potential and influenced its future. He was also that rarest of persons: a government official with vision and vigor.

In 1883 he became the art critic for the magazine *Voltaire*, and was named to the board of the Beaux-Arts (France's cultural administration), becoming its director in 1888. The following year he was appointed Inspector General of France's Provincial Museums and organized the Centennial Exhibition of French Art. He wrote for many journals, editing *L'Image* and collaborating with André Marty to publish *L'Estampe Originale*. From 1902, until his death in 1913, he was executive editor of the influential *Gazette des Beaux Arts*.

Roger Marx deserves to be hailed as the precursor of a modern concept of the fine arts. "We have come to understand that the realm of art extends only to what we see at exhibitions, in museums, and hear in concerts. This, however, is only a very small part of the larger art which binds men together." This Tolstoi quote, which Roger Marx adopted as his own, expressed his real feelings on the subject: Although he wrote and spoke marvelously of painting and sculpture, Roger Marx spent most of his energy to fight for the applied arts. He saw art everywhere—and especially in the streets and in the architecture of the city. He always propagated the cause of printmakers and posterists. Thanks to his enthusiastic support, applied and decorative arts were allowed to be exhibited at the Salon de la Société Nationale in 1891, and again, beginning in 1895, at the Salon des Artistes Français.

Roger Marx's strength was that he not only espoused but actively fought for his ideals. He especially championed unknown or unpopular artists: Degas, Puvis de Chavannes, Fantin-Latour, Gustave Moreau, Rodin (who did a bust of him), Albert Besnard, Eugène Carrière, Ernest Laurent, Maurice Denis, Charles Cottet, and Brangwyn, to name only a few of the artists who benefited from his patronage.

The decorative arts—which he preferred to call *l'art social*—found in him a tireless defender. He fought against the forced segregation of artist and artisan. In a succession of articles he spoke, in turn, of French medallists, the reform of the currency design, the design of the postage stamp, of Gallé, Lalique, Loie Fuller, as well as Jules Chéret and the poster. Indeed, the poster—to him the ultimate *art social*—fascinated him and it is easy to understand why the Chaix printing firm called on his authority and enthusiasm to preface the volumes of *Les Maîtres de l'Affiche*.

Roger Marx did more than any other individual to encourage the acceptance of the poster as a valid artistic expression and a document to be preserved. He practiced what he preached: He was an avid collector of posters and prints and it took two months, from April to June 1914, to auction off his vast collection.

In his yearly preface, Roger Marx did more than write the expected tribute to the poster. Always positive and forward-looking, he outlined, in volumes 4 and 5, his concept for a much-needed Poster Museum which would preserve these fragile documents for future generations. His ideas on the subject had great impact and his plans for this Museum became the starting point for a great discussion on the subject in the magazine *L'Estampe et l'Affiche*.

Eighty years later, when projects for poster museums are being announced and are nearing realization in several countries, the soundness and acuity of Roger Marx's vision is even more firmly established.

Preface by Roger Marx

PREFACE to Volume I (1896), which contains Plates 1-48.

During this "fin de siècle" era which imposes unceasing activity on the brain, streets themselves conspire against the relaxation of the eye, the mind; the ever changing decor which covers the city's walls forcefully draws our attention, and even the busiest, most skeptical passerby must submit to the charm of the sight that has been flung onto his path, follow the spirited arabesque of the design, delight in the variegated flora blooming among the gray stones. The fact is, that to be sure to make an impression and better to convince, Advertising has called upon art for help; it has borrowed the poetry of allegories, it has become image, and its beautiful appearance has bestowed upon it, with unexpected efficiency, the indefeasible right to the esthetes' attention.

Everyone has been able to follow the metamorphosis. The poster of yore, its ugly typography without seductiveness, slow to decipher, has become a veritable art print whose polychromy brightens the eye, whose symbolism is directly understood. What a brilliant fortune for the illustrated poster that a master of a uniquely French style, taste and temperament, Jules Chéret, renewed it and, in fact, recreated it some thirty years ago! It gave rise to critics' studies, commentaries by the proudest writers and found in Ernest Maindron the historiographer of its splendors. Devotees, by the legions, search for it and their portfolios offer the poster the safe haven that keeps and preserves it for posterity.

In France and abroad as well, mural chromolithography has attracted the best artists, those who instinctively possess a decorative vocation as well as the ironists and the mystics, all the poets of imagination and dream. Such eagerness should not come as a surprise; the reasons for it can be found in the infinite resources of the process, in the broadness of the field open to the artist, the exposure given the work by an always animated street, alive with people, where discussions take place and the public's vote is cast.

Some dullards deny the benefits of contact with the common people. They are deluding themselves! Let them read William Morris' decisive argument refuting their thesis in a wonderful lecture. Let them also think about examples from the past. The first Salons, exhibitions of paintings, took place al fresco, under the sky's light. These Salons were at least as good as the present ones. And just as they had done to the Masters of the Poster, they subjected to the judgment of the street the members of the Academy Saint-Luc, "The Gentlemen of the Royal Academy," when in 1673 they exhibited on the Place Dauphine and in the courtyard of the Palais-Royal their "paintings and pieces of sculpture. . .".

This museum in the breeze is a sight now still in existence in the street due to the illustrated poster. It is, I know, a museum created by chance, where the work of genius jostles the mediocre, the exquisite adjoins the vulgar, the witty is placed side by side with the absurd—a museum which renews itself with the suddenness of a transformation scene in a fairy play because the poster has the precarious fate of everything that glitters, from the butterfly to the flower, it gleams in the sun, fades in the mist, dangles sadly in shreds, sways in the wind after a heavy shower or a squall. We would like to retain this view, safeguarding so much charming production from oblivion, but the task of selecting from an ever increasing number of posters has become more and more arduous. Even those who try, find their good intentions hampered by the smallness of the home, the difficulty to display and to preserve these fragile sheets, so delicate when unfurled, so large that the eye can almost never, unless we step back, embrace the entire picture. From there stems the desire to save people the trouble of making a selection and the idea to offer a poster reduced to the size of a print, in every respect faithful to the original, easy to handle, suitable for frequent and quick examination and concurrent enjoyment.

It fell to the Imprimerie Chaix, where Jules Chéret published so many radiant masterpieces, now considered classics, to take the initiative of this publication, to assure its success by means of a selection free from prejudice and a reproduction which is the perfection of the chromolithographic process. Grouped fraternally, the masters of Europe and America will see their most important pages included in this Panthéon of the modern poster and reflect there, according to temperament, climate, race, the infinite diversity of the human genius. Without contradiction, to be successful it would suffice for such a collection to ascertain the day by day progress of a special art, an art in constant evolution, in full efflorescence. But it has a yet higher, more general scope: on these pages, ravished from their ephemeral fate, come to life again the manners and morals, the fashions and tastes, the thousand spectacles of public and private life. At the same time, bringing them together in these pages constitutes a unique and essential repertory for the study of the modern schools, a source of information which the future scholar cannot omit without condemning himself to inexact conclusions on the decorative aspirations and complex tendencies of contemporary esthetics.

15 November 1895.

PREFACE to Volume II (1897), which contains Plates 49-96.

Though it has fallen on *Les Maîtres de l'Affiche* to satisfy the secret wish of devotees whose numbers around the world are legion, we should not celebrate, at the outset of this second year, the success of the first book. Although praise for it is constantly increasing, a tribute would be out of place here and, in addition, would appear to be a bit late. That the innate love for color has had people enjoy the polychromy of these prints, that certain people have recognized in it a valuable document for the history of art and societies; that almost all have begun to consider the collection as the international tribute of original talent—these results have been established for some time. The publication, widely accepted and highly rated, has almost become a classic; and the welcome it has received attests again to the interest shown the poster by the public which alone, it is said, is more spiritual than Voltaire.

During 1896, everything seems to have come together to legitimize and increase this devotion: For instance, the use of novel and unexpected processes; Mr. Paul Desjardins' initiative to bring Puvis de Chavannes' admirable frescoes in the Pantheon to the passerby's view by means of a lithographed transcription [Ed. Note: see PL. 54]; special poster exhibits, opening here and there, sometimes with quasi-official ceremonies as in Rheims, in Dresden's Royal Hall of Prints and Strasbourg's Hohenlohe Museum, sometimes with touching simplicity as in a modest Swiss town called Stein, and also the quality and the number of glorifying studies which have appeared in France, outside of France, everywhere . . .

"The Age of the Poster" that's how, yesterday, the *Revue des Deux Mondes* defined the times we live in. The designation, a happy find, may be maintained if we are not mistaken about the reasons which warrant its use.

The importance accorded mural lithography arises from causes which are not surrounded by any mystery. The progress of civilization has created different conditions of existence; in the course of the centuries, public life has been modified from within and from without; tapestries no longer line the king's path; signs are no longer patiently colored, cut into oak trees or hewn in the stone. Just as society, so the street has been transformed; it no longer witnesses the splendor of royal pomp nor the slow undertakings of the old master painters. The streets' adornment was exceptional, intermittent and unalterable; now it is always present and always renewed. The picturesqueness of narrow alleys has been succeeded by the picturesqueness of broad, variegated modern thoroughfares; it is a scene which also has its beauty and of which the poster is the essential element.

Does it follow that every poster has the privilege to embellish and adorn the wall that receives it? Not so. It is successful only on condition that it meets the laws of mural decoration. This aspect is hardly taken into consideration by the detractors who are so quick to censure the effects of a technique required to realize the purpose of the poster. For instance, the sharply set off arabesques and lines are an integral part of the poster's design, for, without it, the composition would not be legible from a distance and the first glance could not embrace it in its entirety; likewise, the display outdoors, in order to sparkle in the glaring light of day, demands just as imperiously the use of fairly brilliant colors.

Besides the technique, the inspiration and the hierarchy of the subject matter has been incriminated. Haven't people dared to accuse the French poster of being incapable of seriousness and nobility? This would be to overstate the paradox and to refuse to recognize that many a masterpiece is profoundly marked by these two characteristics. When the occasion demands it, the poster does not fail to inspire charity, admiration, labor, incite one to take stock of oneself; but it also knows to be cajoling, graceful and light, and we would really deserve to be pitied if the essential talent of the race had suddenly been abolished and if charm, elegance and joy ceased to find exponents and poets in the land of Watteau, Fragonard and Chéret.

Far from becoming alarmed, let's be grateful to the poster for having fostered the survival of a national tradition and for possessing the sound frankness of a folk art of which it is the highest expression. It is for such reasons that its future is happily assured and promising and that its present success is neither banal nor a passing phase; it will last as long as the economic and social evolution which gave birth to the poster; it will persist as long as humanity will ask of art to speak to the imagination, to entertain us and to restore equanimity to our lives.

15 November 1896.

PREFACE to Volume III (1898), which contains Plates 97-144.

It seems that until now people have not become precisely aware of the role which has fallen upon the illustrated poster in the renaissance of ornamental arts. Economists, busy with figures and statistics, have recorded, in passing, the existence of a new industry. As for our historians, almost all have been content to paraphrase J.K. Huysmans' initial remarks on the changing aspect of our modern thoroughfare. No doubt, it would already be beautiful to have wrested the street from the gray uniformity of the perfectly straight line of its buildings, to have flung on the walls the illusion of life, the flaming brightness of color. But the action of the poster is not limited, as valuable as this may be, to such an advantage and we would be remiss to see in it only an invitation and a pleasure for the eyes of the stroller in search of beauty.

Since the World's Fair of 1889, the twofold interest of an important event and an educational aspect marked the works of Chéret, assembled by the Imprimerie Chaix in the Palace of Liberal Arts: the supremacy of the master shone with incomparable brightness. At the same time the critics evaluated the benefits of such lessons and predicted for the near future a regeneration of good taste and invention. A whole movement of progress could come about. Let the decorators wrest from the poster the secrets of a rational technique and the virtues of a spontaneous inspiration. It would not be long before the intimacy of our homes would also be covered and brightened up by the colors of happiness; and it would spell the end of dreary dwellings and out-of-date environments amidst which the days follow each other monotonously.

Nevertheless, the evolution of the arts, like that of ideas, does not follow this hasty path. In the beginning there simply was imitation, the assimilation of the poster to a model, a cartoon: the crafts transform it into fabric or again, in the form of stained glass, it takes up a less ephemeral existence; and then, following this example, the binding, the bookcover, the music title sheet and commercial printing of all type was renovated. We are astonished that the scope of such suggestive council could have eluded some, notably the producers of printed paper; and look at the effect of their negligence: longing becomes impatient, doesn't grant a delay; as a consequence of the shortage of truly embellishing wallpaper, the poster becomes the familiar tapestry of the wall, it finds in the house the security of a haven and the tribute of a daily admiration; it becomes the essence of the home's ornament just as it had become the decor of the street.

As usual, such a brilliant success had to give birth to envy and stir up rivalries. The poster has seen the creation—to contend for its favored status—of a picture-making industry among which there are many masterpieces: Chéret's glistening allegories, Grasset's evocations of women, Rivière's disquieting landscapes. But neither the unexpected format nor the absence of letters, and not even the care and appropriate execution could lead to a change of classification by the iconograph; these apartment prints remain for him varieties of mural colorlithography and their success proves that the poster's beneficent mission is being accomplished, is still going on far and wide.

It has expanded into the school. In Switzerland, the classroom walls are covered with railroad timetables where the illustration reveals the geographic features of a region as well as the picturesque style of its old costumes. To the pupils' watchful eye, the British have proposed huge colored posters whose subjects are taken from the Bible, legend and country life. In the past it behooved Mr. Moreau-Nélaton to endow our French schools with color compositions of the most highminded and sound inspiration; but if Viollet-le-Duc's wish has obtained satisfaction on both sides of the Channel, isn't it that here and there the wall picture has become identical, as to technique, with the illustrated poster which Viollet-le-Duc had heralded, defined, desired, in the already distant past, when he demanded for the youth, "pictures of the diverse works of the fields and the crafts, treated in conformity with the original methods, with elementary coloration, without richness of form. . ."?

Understood by people of all ages, loved by the masses, the poster speaks to the universal spirit: it has come to satisfy new aspirations and this love of beauty which the education of taste spreads and develops without interruption. On the outside and in the home it has replaced the paintings which used to be visible at the doorstep of palaces, under the vaults of cloisters and churches; it is the roving, ephemeral picture that an era, infatuated with vulgarization and eager for change, called for. Its art has neither less meaning nor less prestige than the art of the fresco; only those who are imbued with the qualifications required of any ornamental enterprise are successful. But while the essential and secular laws of decoration are almost everywhere disregarded, violated at will, respect for them has been maintained by the masters of the poster; because of it the success of their effort and the authority of their influence is justified. To meditate on their works is to hasten the return of basic originality to the depraved inspiration, to stimulate the free expansion of inventive faculties; it is also to rise to the heights of knowledge to the immutable principles which have, at all times, governed the arts of decor and of life.

10 November 1897.

PREFACE to Volume IV (1899), which contains Plates 145-192.

It would be a great mistake to attribute the success of the poster only to the progress of an art that is in perfect harmony with the needs of modern civilization; the esteem in which it is held now can also be explained by the evolution of ideas and by a belated renunciation of biased arbitrary classifications. For many years, the shackle of hierarchies deflected the attention from the poster to arts reputed to be "major" or "higher"—outside of those there was no salvation. Even more, the utility aspect appeared to be a cause for contempt, a sign of degradation. How can we hope for some interest in a social art and sympathy for some ephemeral pictures destined for the street, from such a deceived public opinion? When the poster was being called in question, people treated it with ironic benevolence, almost excusing themselves for talking about it.

In this manner, the scope of the poster remained for a long time unrecognized. Educators did not see in it a valuable and unconscious tool of esthetic schooling, like the medal or coin; scholars and learned people turned their backs to it as well, considering it not dignified enough for their serious writings. Rather than to cry out pessimistically, let's leaf through the most recent dictionaries of art: neither Jules Adeline in his *Lexique*, nor Paul Rouaix, nor Henry Harvard, in their huge special encyclopedias, think of studying or defining the poster. So much contempt or neglect is surprising and happily without reason; the writer loses an opportunity to inform with exactness on the state of engraving and decoration at the end of the Nineteenth Century.

We must sweep away these rank prejudices which obscure good judgment; the time of disdain and silence is past; our claim is based on established facts. The poster is like the print in technique and it is second to none, including painting, as to the richness of its impact, a fact we must repeat mercilessly. As early as 1880, J.K. Huysmans, a critic whose perspicacity is infallible, "discovered more talent in one Chéret poster than in most paintings of the Salon." And everyone spoke out and considered the remark revolutionary! It has, nevertheless, the evident force of an axiom. The quality of a work is independent of the process of expression; the means are as good as the artist. In the present case it pertains to works intended to variegate the walls of the buildings; whether the colored picture is indoors or exposed to the open air, painted or lithographed, preeminence is promised to works which do not fail in their mission to beautify.

Now, the poster is decorative or it doesn't exist at all; as for the author of posters, practice preserves and develops the talent for illustration and that is why the ornamental virtues of his posters are a quality shared by all his other works. Moreover, palette in hand, Chéret, Willette and Toulouse-Lautrec have pursued their glorious careers with equal mastery. Who then would dare deny the reciprocity of success when the painter, for his part, has made himself a mural lithographer?

More so than any of its predecessors, our generation has become concerned with the esthetics of the street. We hear about speeches, conferences and initiatives to save our cities from the imminent threat of vandalism and uglifying uniformity. We ought to applaud the sound alarm of cultivated people of good taste. What a noble concern to muse about public art and to save the works of the past which time and man's folly have not destroyed! I wish only that the neophytes' gratefulness would extend to the painter-printmakers who have, as early as yesterday, adorned the surroundings of our activities, and that an equal zeal demand the preservation of only those works which have contributed to give our modern streets their original appearance and hours of beauty.

This collection offers a selection which proves the diversity and brilliance of today's talents. But other duties, outside a publisher's realm, are incumbent upon the State: Our Museums' Print Rooms must collect, shelter and transmit to posterity the entire poster production of our time. In this manner, day by day, a documentary collection will be formed which will be called upon to testify about the art and life of our times; thus a museum will be founded which in the beginning will not escape ridicule, yet one which posterity will demand and open, logically, inevitably: The Modern Museum of the Illustrated Poster.

15 November 1898.

PREFACE to Volume V (1900), which contains Plates 193-240.

At the end of the journey, it is without boasting and without self-satisfaction that we look at the road travelled and the distance covered. This look back takes on the significance of a soul searching; it allows us to evaluate whether the effort has attained its precise and clearly stated goal.

Everyone remembers the motives which determined the publication that now comes to an end: it was published at the right time to exalt an art that, some thought, had reached its high point, which all believed to be at a stage of exceptional efflorescence. For five years, it was the task of *Les Maîtres de l'Affiche* to reveal the state of mural chromolithography at the end of the century; in addition, by letting the masterpieces emerge from the flood of the current production we have administered a lesson of high eclecticism and established favorable points of reference for the orientation of taste. To the documentary attraction has been added the edifying example of a selection made for posterity among the confused creation of a period. The lustre of the present collection has no other origin: it would be tarnished the moment the tares would be mixed with the wheat and pieces of doubtful merit would usurp undeserved consecration. This disgrace of a slow decline, the editors did not want to suffer; it seemed to them more appropriate to limit their work than to desecrate it by continuing it beyond measure, against all reason.

The initial promises of the program, haven't they been realized, and more! Nowadays the former prejudice has faded away. There is no more doubt as to the rightful place of the poster in the history of French decorative arts. But look at the fruits of such a teaching: the interest taken in the reproduction of the most beautiful mural images has suggested the wish to preserve for posterity the originals from which the national movement obtained a legitimate dividend of glory, and the logic of reasoning induced us last year to call for a Museum of the Modern Poster.

As soon as we announced our demand, a special edition of the magazine, *L'Estampe et l'Affiche* (March 15 and May 15, 1899), hastened to open an inquiry; artists and amateurs have been invited to express their opinion. The results of the consultation should be kept in mind. On the principle of the project and its opportuneness there were few or hardly any differences of opinion; on the other hand the display, protection and communication of the posters did not fail to stir up some difficulties. It will be easy to overcome these as long as we are aware of the role assigned to the wished for foundation. Let it be a department of the future Musée des Arts Décoratifs, an annex of the Bibliothèque Nationale, or a separate building. We imagine it as deriving its features from the Cabinet d'estampes as well as the Salon and decorated accordingly on the outside: against the walls a periodically changed choice of famous posters, classics; on shelves reaching up to the top, arranged according to artist and date, the works of the unknown and the famous. The care of a volunteer curator would not be missing from the collection and an insignificant amount of credit would be enough to assure its future, once the building has been ceded. The scrupulous intent not to leave anything out would make it advisable and necessary to mount on cloth each piece, on arrival. Thus, the posters could be handled without risk and without damage. The preceding defines, in detail, the economics of an essentially viable museum which will soon be rich and complete due to gifts, bequests, and the fund of copies deposited with the State in accordance with law.

On what authority could one still refuse the poster the respect rightfully gained by the print to which it has been assimilated? Art could only gain from an equal and equitable treatment. Nothing is more likely to flatter and stimulate the artist than the conviction that his work will survive the capriciousness of an ephemeral exhibition. Let's not fabricate unnecessary worries: the urgency of such archives will soon be evident to all, when the feverishness of ever increasing advertising will have multiplied for the talented the opportunities to make their mark and to be applauded; because, in spite of the pessimists, the illustrator of the street ought not to stand in fear of unemployment in the future. . . It is without apprehension that the waning century entrusts the new era with the destiny and glory of the illustrated poster.

1 November 1899.

NUMERICAL TABLE OF REPRODUCTIONS

The listing here is that provided by the publisher, Chaix, at the beginning of each year's compendium. Some changes and additions have been made: We have translated the text of the non-English posters. For 64 of the 240 regular plates, no dates were given; we have placed actual or approximate dates for each of these as well. Unless otherwise indicated, all posters are French. Printer's name follows city where published.

The size given was in centimeters and the series began with height preceding width in all cases except one of the plates in the first volume, and then erratically but gradually shifted to width before height (which happens to be our own preference). However, for the sake of uniformity, we have given all sizes as height first, width second. And we have added the equivalent size in inches, to the nearest half inch. For the most part, the sizes given by Chaix are those of the entire sheet of printed paper, not just the image area.

The sequence is that of the original edition, with the exception of the placement of the special "bonus" plates which subscribers received (two each of the first two years, four each of the last three years). The original sequence of these special plates (which were unnumbered but which we have numbered "SP.PL.#1 to #16) was as follows: Sp.Pl.#1 came before Pl.1, #2 came after 24, #3 after 48, #4 after 72, #5 after 96, #6 after 108, #7 after 120, #8 after 132, #9 after 144, #10 after 156, #11 after 168, #12 after 180, #13 after 192, #14 after 204, #15 after 216, #16 after 228. As can be seen, a special plate by Chéret started each year's series and also ended the last one.

Except for the translation, addition of inch-measurements and dates where missing, all the information listed here is that provided by Chaix. Only a few obvious errors have been corrected, i.e., Plate 208 was listed as a Czech poster when it is Hungarian; Maxfield Parrish's name was misspelled on Plate 123; the size of Plate 107 had been given as 75 × 95 cm and this was corrected to 180 × 75 cm; the description of plate 105 was that of another poster, not shown; the only anonymously-credited poster, Plate 176, is in fact the work of Vaclav Oliva, etc.

1896

PL.1. JULES CHÉRET	Poster for Job cigarette paper. 1895. Paris, Chaix. 124 × 88 cm/49 × 34.5 in
PL.2. TOULOUSE-LAUTREC	Poster for the Divan Japonais cabaret. 1892. Paris, Ancourt. 81 × 62 cm/32 × 24.5 in
PL.3. JULIUS PRICE	English poster for Daly's Theatre. 1895. Paris, Dupont. 216 × 150 cm/85.5 × 59 in
PL.4. DUDLEY HARDY	English poster for "A Gaiety Girl." 1894. London, Waterlow & Sons. 76 × 50 cm/30 × 20 in
PL.5. JULES CHÉRET	Poster for the Punch Grassot "available in all great Cafés." 1895. Paris, Chaix. 124 × 88 cm/49 × 34.5 in
PL.6. H.-G. IBELS	Poster for the illustrated weekly "L'Escarmouche" containing drawings by Anouetin, Ibels, Lautrec, etc. 1893. Paris, Verneau. 65 × 50 cm/25.5 × 20 in
PL.7. GEORGES MEUNIER	Poster for Frossard's Cavour cigars. 1895. Paris, Chaix. 246 × 88 cm/97 × 34.5 in

PL.8. LOUIS RHEAD	American poster for "The Sun" newspaper. 1894. New York. 116 × 76 cm/45.5 × 30 in
PL.9. JULES CHÉRET	Poster for the "Carnaval 1896" production at the Théâtre de l'Opéra. 1896. Paris, Chaix. 124 × 88 cm/49 × 34.5 in
PL.10. GEORGES DE FEURE	Poster for the 5th Art Exhibit held at the Salon des Cent. 1894. Paris, Bourgerie. 64 × 43 cm/25 × 17 in
PL.11. LUCIEN LEFÈVRE	Poster for Charles Gravier's Cacao Lacté (cocoa with milk) "superior to all known chocolates and cocoas." 1893. Paris, Chaix. 124 × 88 cm/49 × 34.5 in
PL.12. ARMAND RASSENFOSSE	Belgian poster for Grande Brasserie Van Velsen, Bornhem. 1894. Liège, Auguste Bénard. 73 × 52 cm/29 × 20.5 in
PL.13. JULES CHÉRET	A new poster for Saxoléine, "an extra white, deodorized, non-flammable safety kerosene available in 5 liter sealed canisters." 1896. Paris, Chaix. 124 × 88 cm/49 × 34.5 in
PL.14. WILLETTE	Poster for the pantomime "L'Enfant Prodigue" (The Return of the Prodigal Child) for the music publisher Biardot. 1890. Paris, Marx. 93 × 66 cm/36.5 × 26 in
PL.15. CAZALS	Poster for the 7th Exhibit at the Salon des Cent. In the foreground a faithful portrait of the poet Verlaine; behind him is Jean Moréas. 1894. Paris, Bourgerie. 61 × 40 cm/24 × 16 in
PL.16. BEGGARSTAFF	English poster for "Harper's Magazine." 1895. Netherfield, Stafford & Co. 220 × 200 cm/86.5 × 79 in
PL.17. JULES CHÉRET	New poster for the Palais de Glace. 1896. Paris, Chaix. 124 × 88 cm/49 × 34.5 in
PL.18. EUGÈNE GRASSET	Poster for the dry goods store "A la Place Clichy" which is "number one in the world for its oriental imports." 1891. Paris, de Malherbe. 140 × 84
PL.19. FERDINAND BAC	Poster for Yvette Guilbert's concert at the Scala. 1893. Paris, Chaix. 213 × 88cm/84 × 34.5 in
PL.20. EDWARD PENFIELD	American poster for "Harper's" magazine. 1894. 49 × 35 cm/19.5 × 14 in
PL.21. JULES CHÉRET	Poster for the pantomime ballet "L'Arc-en-Ciel," performed at the Folies-Bergere. 1893. Paris, Chaix. 124 × 88 cm/49 × 34.5 in
PL.22. LUCIEN MÉTIVET	Poster for the appearance of Eugénie Buffet at the Ambassadeurs. 1893. Paris, Verneau. 118 × 80 cm/42.5 × 31.5 in
PL.23 MAURICE RÉALIER-DUMAS	Poster for the "Incandescence par le Gaz" (Auer system). 1892. Paris, Chaix. 176 × 62 cm/69.5 × 24.5 in
PL.24 MAURICE GREIFFENHAGEN	English poster for the weekly magazine "Illustrated Pall Mall Budget." 1894. London, W.H. Smith. 200 × 150 cm/79 × 59 in
PL.25. JULES CHÉRET	Poster for Alcazar d'Été's "Lidia." 1895. Paris, Chaix. 124 × 88 cm/49 × 34.5 in
PL.26. BOUTET DE MONVEL	Poster for Docteur Pierre's tootpaste. 1894. Paris, Devarenne. 82 × 61 cm/32 × 22.5 in
PL.27. ALPHONSE MUCHA	Poster for Sarah Bernhardt's appearance in "Gismonda" at the Théâtre de la Renaissance. 1894. Paris, Lemercier. 211 × 69 cm/83 × 27 in

PL.28. ED. DUYCK & A. CRESPIN Belgian poster for the Ferme de Frahinfaz, on the Hippodrome des Art road near Spa. "Accommodations for riders and pedestrians. Fork-and-knife lunches, fresh milk, real Faro beer from Brussels and English beers." 1894. Brussels, Van Buggenhout. 118 × 89 cm/ 42.5 × 35 in

Pl.29 JULES CHÉRET Poster for Quinquina Dubonnet, an "apéritif available in all Cafés." 1895. Paris. Chaix. 124 × 88 cm/49 × 34.5 in

PL.30. A. GUILLAUME Poster for the Théâtre de l'Ambigu's production of "Gigolette." 1894. Paris, Camis. 190 × 125 cm/75 × 49 in

PL.31. GEORGES MEUNIER Poster for the Western Railroad Company (Chemins de fer de l'Ouest). "Round trip tickets at reduced prices. Bulletins, booklets and guide books containing useful information concerning rates for excursions, resorts, etc., may be obtained free of charge from the company upon request." 1896. Paris, Chaix. 105 × 79 cm/41.5 × 31 in

PL.32. CHARLES H. WOODBURY American poster for "The Century" magazine, published in New York. 1895. New York. 48 × 30 cm/19 × 12 in

PL.33. JULES CHÉRET Poster for the Théâtrophone company. 1890. Paris, Chaix. 124 × 88 cm/49 × 34.5 in

PL.34. T.A. STEINLEN Poster for the opera "Hellé" performed at the Théâtre national de l'Opéra. 1896. Paris, Verneau. 80 × 60 cm/31.5 × 23.5 in

PL.35. PAL Poster for "Grand Ballet Brighton" at the Theatre Olympia. 1893. Paris, Dupont. 122 × 80 cm/48 × 31.5 in

PL.36. ARTHUR W. DOW American poster for the magazine "Modern Art" published in Boston. 1895. Boston, Prang. 54 × 39 cm/21 × 15.5 in

PL.37. JULES CHÉRET Poster for the Musée Grévin's production of "Les Coulisses de l'Opéra" (Behind the Scenes at the Opera). 1891. Paris, Chaix. 243 × 87 cm/95.5 × 34 in

PL.38. PIERRE BONNARD Poster for the magazine "La Revue Blanche." The price and frequency of publication listed on the poster have since been changed. The magazine appears bi-monthly, contains 50 pages and costs 60 centimes. 1894. Paris, Ancourt. 62 × 80 cm/24.5 × 31.5 in

PL.39. GASTON NOURY Poster for the Grandes Fêtes (Celebrations) at the Tuileries. "For the indigents of France and Russia . . . Please consult the special poster for the program." 1892. Paris, Herold. 99 × 139 cm/39 × 54.5 in

PL.40. HENRI MEUNIER Belgian poster for the "Concerts Ysaye" in Brussels. 1895. Brussels, Goossens. 89 × 125 cm/35 × 49 in

PL.41. JULES CHÉRET Poster for the "Pantomimes Lumineuses" production at the Musée Grévin. 1892. Paris, Chaix. 124 × 88 cm/49 × 34.5 in

PL.42. EUGÈNE GRASSET Poster for the Librairie Romantique, a collection of 12-page serialized books, featuring the works of "romantic and Gothic prose writers, poets, orators, musicians, painters, printmakers, watercolorists, etc." 1887. Paris, Bognard. 128 × 90 cm/51.5 × 35.5 in

PL.43. WILLETTE Poster for Cacao Van Houten. 1893. Paris, Belfond. 193 × 67 cm/76 × 26.5 in

PL.44. WILLIAM CARQUEVILLE American poster for "Lippincott's" magazine, published in Philadelphia. 1895. 48 × 31.5 cm/19 × 12.5 in

PL.45. JULES CHÉRET	Poster for Félicien Champsaur's novel, "L'Amant des Danseuses" which is "sold at all bookstores" for 3.50 francs per copy. 1892. Paris, Chaix. 124 × 88 cm/49 × 34.5 in
PL.46. T.A. STEINLEN	Poster for the sketches titled "Mothu and Doria". 1893. Paris, Impressions Artistique. 130 × 94 cm/51 × 37 in
PL.47. FIRMIN BOUISSET	Poster for Chocolat Menier. 1892. Paris, Camis. 130 × 94 cm/51 × 37 in
PL.48. DUDLEY HARDY	English poster for the Savoy Theatre's production of Burnand and Sullivan's "The Chieftain." 1895. London, Waterlow. 75 × 49 cm/ 29.5 × 19.5 in
SP.PL.1. JULES CHÉRET	Original design for the cover of "Les Maîtres de l'Affiche." Collector's proof, red plus tint, without text.
SP.PL.2. JULES CHÉRET	Original design for "Les Maîtres de l'Affiche." Collector's proof, red plus tint, without text.
SP.PL.3. JULES CHÉRET	Original design for "Les Maîtres de l'Affiche." Collector's proof, executed in 3 colors ("trois crayons"), without text.
SP.PL.4. WILLETTE	Original design for "Les Maîtres de l'Affiche" titled "Impatience." Collector's proof, in crayon, without text.

1897

PL.49. JULES CHÉRET	Poster for the newspaper "Le Courrier Francais." 1891. Paris, Chaix. 124 × 88 cm/49 × 34.5 in
PL.50. EUGÈNE GRASSET	Poster for the "Fêtes de Paris." Announcing: "Gala performance at the Opéra National, Tuesday, January 26, 1886. The History of the Theater. Reconstruction of numerous theater acts from antiquty to the present time." 1885. Paris, Appel. 129 × 93 cm/51 × 36.5 in
PL.51. J.-L. FORAIN	Poster for the Second Bicycle Show held at the Palais de l'Industrie. 1894. Paris, Herold. 90 × 205 cm/35.5 × 80.5 in
PL.52. WILL BRADLEY	American poster, "When Hearts are Trumps." To announce Tom Hall's volume of verse. "The artist's composition suggests love." 1890. Chicago. 44 × 36 cm/17.5 × 14 in
PL.53. JULES CHÉRET	Poster for the Bal du Moulin Rouge. "Performances every evening and Sunday afternoon, special performances on Wednesdays and Saturdays." 1889. Paris, Chaix. 124 × 88 cm/49 × 34.5 in
PL.54. PUVIS DE CHAVANNES	Poster for the Union for Moral Action, depicting "L'Enfance de Sainte Geneviève." In this reproduction of the fresco of the Panthéon, the text below first panel reads: "From early age, St. Geneviève gave signs of ardent piety, always in prayer. She was admired by all those who saw her." Text below third panel: "In the year CDXXIX St. Germain d'Auxerre and St. Loup de Troyes went to England to fight against Pélage's heresy. Near Nanterre, St. Germain notices a child in the crowd which he believes touched by the divine seal. He questions her and predicts to her parents that she will be called upon to play a sacred role. This child was St. Geneviève, the Patron Saint of Paris." 1896. Paris, Lemercier. 150 × 325 cm/59 × 128 in
PL.55. LUCIEN LEFÈVRE	Poster for Electricine, luxury lighting. 1895. Paris, Chaix. 124 × 88 cm/49 × 34.5 in
PL.56. HYNAÏS	Czech poster for the Exposition Ethnographique Tcheco-Slave de Prague: "People and country, language, songs, dances, costumes and customs, architecture, popular art, etc. Prague in the 16th century." 1894. Prague, Neubert. 125 × 136 cm/49 × 53.5 in

PL.57. JULES CHÉRET	Poster for the First Great Masked Ball held at the Théâtre de l'Opéra, Saturday, January 30, 1897. 1896. Paris, Chaix. 124 × 88 cm/49 × 34.5 in
PL.58. MOREAU-NÉLATON	Poster for the second exhibition of Women's Art. 1895. Paris, Verneau. 116 × 70 cm/45.5 × 27.5 in
PL.59. AUGUSTE DONNAY	Belgian poster for the International Choral Song Contest organized by the City of Liège. 1895. Liège, Jaspar. 205 × 135 cm/80.5 × 53 in
PL.60. ALICE R. GLENNY	American poster for Women's Edition of the "Buffalo Courier." 1895. Buffalo, Courier. 62 × 37 cm/24.5 × 14.5 in
PL.61. JULES CHÉRET	Poster for the Racetrack at the Hippodrome, Porte Maillot, Paris. "A New Sport. Grand Prize: A river of diamonds valued at 20,000 Francs." 1890. Paris, Chaix. 124 × 88 cm/49 × 34.5 in
PL.62. GEORGES MEUNIER	Poster for the "Trianon Concert" variety show in the garden of the Elysée Montmartre: 1895. Paris, Chaix. 124 × 88 cm
PL.63. BEGGARSTAFF	English poster for the Lyceum Theatre's production of "Don Quixote." 1896. London. 213 × 198 cm/84 × 78 in
PL.64. A. DE RIQUER	Spanish poster for the Third Barcelona Exhibition of Fine and Industrial Arts, to be held from April to June 1896. 1895. Barcelona, Thomas. 99 × 150 cm/39 × 59 in
PL.65. JULES CHÉRET	Poster for the Jardin de Paris at Champs-Elysées. "Spectacle. Concert. Evening Show. Ball every Tuesday, Wednesday, Friday and Saturday." 1890. Paris, Chaix. 124 × 88 cm/49 × 34.5 in
PL.66. F. HUGO D'ALÉSI	Poster for the Centennial of Lithography exhibition held at the Galerie Rapp. 1895. Paris, Courmont. 158 × 115 cm/62 × 45 in
PL.67. JOSEPH SATTLER	German poster for the art magazine "Pan." "Pan as gardener personifies the magazine. On the right, agricultural implements, symbols of art. When he awakens the God is surprised and charmed to see the flower he so carefully cultivated. The pistils and the stamen form the name of the magazine and the date." 1895. Berlin, Frisch. 35 × 28 cm/14 × 11 in
PL.68. OTTO FISCHER	German poster for the Saxon Crafts and Art Exhibition at Dresden in 1896. "A view of the Old City." 1896. Dresden, Hoffmann. 69 × 102 cm/27 × 40 in
PL.69. JULES CHÉRET	Poster for Emile Zola's novel, "La Terre" (The Earth). 1889. Paris, Chaix. 245 × 88 cm/96.5 × 34.5 in
PL.70. CARAN D'ACHE	Poster for the Russian Exhibit on the Champ-de-Mars. 1895. Paris. Hérold. 139 × 90 cm/55 × 35.5 in
PL.71. LÉO GAUSSON	Poster for Figaro, "the only antiseptic detergent." 1893. Paris, Verneau. 121 × 79 cm/47.5 × 31 in
PL.72. GIOVANNI MATALONI	Italian poster for the Incandescenza a Gas (an incandescent light using the Auer system). 1895. Rome, Istituto Cartografico Italiano. 149 × 100 cm/58.5 × 39.5 in
PL.73. JULES CHÉRET	Poster for Loie Fuller's appearance at the Folies-Bergère. 1893. Paris, Chaix. 124 × 88 cm/49 × 34.5 in
PL.74. CARLOZ SCHWABE	Poster for the Exhibition of the Rose+Croix. "Purety has broken her terrestrial chains. Faith reaches out to help her cross the steps of mystical flowers that lead to Heaven, while ignorant Humanity, bogged down in a mire, looks on enviously." 1892. Paris, Draeger & Lesieur. 191 × 82 cm/75 × 32 in

PL.75. ROEDEL	Poster for the Moulin de la Galette. 1896. Paris, Malfeyt. 130 × 91 cm/51 × 36 in
PL.76. M.L. STOWELL	American poster for George Humphrey's bookstore, Rochester, N.Y. 1896. Rochester, Peerless. 64 × 43 cm/25 × 17 in
PL.77. JULES CHÉRET	Poster for Vin Mariani. 1894. Paris, Chaix. 124 × 88 cm/49 × 34.5 in
PL.78. H.-G. IBELS	Poster for Mévisto. 1895. Paris, Delanchy. 168 × 120 cm/66 × 47 in
PL.79. A.G. MORROW	English poster for the Comedy Theatre's "The New Woman." 1894. Belfast, David Allen. 62 × 47 cm/24.5 × 18.5 in
PL.80. FERNAND TOUSSAINT	Belgian poster for "Le Sillon," the Painter's Circle. "Glory, personified by a young winged girl, amidst the wheat, a sheaf in one hand, a sickle in the other, harvests flowers for the chosen." 1895. Brussels, Rycker. 110 × 90 cm/43 × 35.5 in
PL.81. JULES CHÉRET	Poster for the weekly "Pan." c.1875. Paris, J. Cheret. 85 × 64 cm/33.5 × 25 in
PL.82. TOULOUSE-LAUTREC	Poster for the bi-monthly magazine, "La Revue Blanche." 1895. Paris, Ancourt. 128 × 93 cm/51 × 36.5 in
PL.83. H. GERBAULT	Poster for Carpentier Chocolat. c.1895. Paris, Courmont. 130 × 95 cm/51 × 37.5 in
PL.84. PAUL FISCHER	Danish poster for the exhibition of Artistic Posters of Wilhelm Söborg. c.1895. Copenhagen, Soborg. 82 × 60 cm/32 × 23.5 in
PL.85. JULES CHÉRET	Poster for Redoute des Etudiants (a student's ball) at the Closerie des Lilas. 1894. Paris, Chaix. 124 × 75 cm/49 × 29.5 in
PL.86. MISTI	Poster for Cycles Gladiator. 1895. Paris, Appel. 148 × 100 cm/58 × 39.5 in
PL.87. FRANK HAZENPLUG	American poster for Chicago poster exhibition titled "Living Posters." 1896. Chicago, Stone & Kimball. 70 × 52 cm/27.5 × 20.5 in
PL.88. PRIVAT-LIVEMONT	Belgian poster for the Casino of Cabourg, "only 5 hours from Paris." 1896. Asnières, Leménil. 75 × 110 cm/29.5 × 43 in
PL.89. JULES CHÉRET	Poster for a Charity Ball to benefit the Society to Help the Families of Ship-Wrecked Sailors. 1890. Paris, Chaix. 124 × 88 cm/49 × 34.5 in
PL.90. LUCIEN LEFÈVRE	Poster for the Jacquot brand of shoe polish. 1894. Paris, Chaix. 176 × 124 cm/69 × 49 in
PL.91. A. CRESPIN	Belgian poster for the architect Paul Hankar. c.1896. Brussels, Mertens. 54 × 40 cm/21 × 16 in
PL.92. DUDLEY HARDY	English poster for Abbott, the shoe manufacturer. c.1895. London, Waterlow. 295 × 195 cm/116 × 76.5 in
PL.93. JULES CHÉRET	Poster for Camille Stéfani. 1896. Paris, Chaix. 124 × 88 cm/49 × 34.5 in
PL.94. ALPHONSE MUCHA	Poster for the 20th Exposition at the Salon des Cent. 1896. Paris, Chaix. 64 × 43 cm/25 × 17 in
PL.95. T.A. STEINLEN	Poster for pure, sterilized milk from the Vingeanne. 1894. Paris, Verneau. 140 × 100 cm/55 × 39.5 in
PL.96. HYLAND ELLIS	English poster for "The Gay Parisienne." c.1896. London, Waterlow. 220 × 194 cm/86.5 × 76.5 in

1898

PL.97. JULES CHÉRET	Poster for an exhibition of drawings and paintings by A. Willette. 1888. Paris, Chaix. 124 × 88 cm/49 × 34.5 in
PL.98. EUGÈNE GRASSET	Poster for Grasset's exhibition at the Salon des Cent. 1894. Paris, Malherbe. 61 × 41 cm/24 × 16 in
PL.99. ETHEL REED	American poster for the novel "Miss Traumerei." 1895. Boston. 56 × 35 cm/22 × 14 in
PL.100. VACLAV OLIVA	Czech poster for an exhibit at the Topic Salon in Prague. c.1896. Prague, Neubert. 110 × 82 cm/43 × 32.5 in
PL.101. JULES CHÉRET	Poster for the Flower Show at Bagnères de Luchon. 1890. Paris, Chaix. 124 × 88 cm/49 × 34.5 in
PL.102. H.-G. IBELS	Poster for Pierrefort, "drawings, paintings and art posters." 1897. Paris, Verneau. 63 × 81 cm/25 × 32 in
PL.103. J.-A. GRÜN	Poster for the Café Riche. "Where do they take her? To the Violin" in the Cafe Riche on the Boulevard des Italiens. 1897. Paris, Bourgerie. 126 × 92 cm/49.5 × 36 in
PL.104. PRIVAT-LIVEMONT	Belgian poster for Absinthe Robette. 1896. Brussels, Goffart. 111 × 83 cm/43.5 × 32.5 in
PL.105. JULES CHÉRET	Poster for the First Masked Ball at the Theatre de l'Opera, January 22, 1898. 1897. Paris, Chaix. 124 × 88 cm/49 × 34.5 in
PL.106. BOUTET DE MONVEL	Poster for the operetta "La Petite Poucette." 1891. Paris, Marx. 80 × 58 cm/31.5 × 23 in
PL.107. BEGGARSTAFF	English poster for the play "Hamlet." 1894. 180 × 75 cm/71 × 29.5 in
PL.108 ÉMILE BERCHMANS	Belgian poster for the Salon of 1896 in the City of Liège sponsored by the Association to Encourage the Fine Arts. 1896. Liège, Bénard. 86 × 125 cm/34 × 49 in
PL.109. JULES CHÉRET	Poster for Quinquina Dubonnet, "an Apéritif available in all the Cafés." 1895. Paris, Chaix. 124 × 88 cm/49 × 34.5 in
PL.110. TOULOUSE-LAUTREC	Poster for Jane Avril's appearance at the Jardin de Paris. 1893. Paris, Chaix. 130 × 94 cm/51 × 37 in
PL.111. RÉALIER-DUMAS	Poster for Mumm champagne. 1895. Paris, Chaix. 176 × 62 cm/69.5 × 24.5 in
PL.112. C.H. WOODBURY	American poster for an exhibition in Boston of works of the Society of Painters in Water Color of Holland. 1895. Boston, Forbes. 59 × 46 cm/23 × 18 in
PL.113. JULES CHÉRET	Poster for Emilienne d'Alençon's appearance at the Folies-Bergère. 1893. Paris, Chaix. 83 × 60 cm/32.5 × 23.5 in
PL.114. ALPHONSE MUCHA	Poster for the play "Lorenzaccio," starring Sarah Bernhardt at the Theatre de la Renaissance. 1896. Paris, Champenois. 207 × 77 cm/ 81.5 × 30.5 in
PL.115. EDWARD PENFIELD	American poster for "Harper's" magazine. 1896. 45 × 30 cm/18 × 12 in
PL.116. H. EVENEPOEL	Belgian poster for the publication "Antwerp and its Exposition." It is "a superb, illustrated, publication; price 1 Franc" and contains "40 pages of text and drawings by the best-known Belgian artists, plus 5 book plates and multi-colored cover." c.1895. Brussels, Goossens. 124 × 90 cm/49 × 35.5 in

PL.117. JULES CHÉRET	Poster for the illustrated edition of the "Works of Rabelais." The quote at bottom left reads: "It is better to write about laughter than about tears, for laughing comes naturally to man. Live Happily." 1895. Paris, Chaix. 244 × 88 cm/96 × 34.5 in
PL.118. MOREAU-NÉLATON	Poster for the passion play, "The Nativity" performed with songs and "tableaux vivants." 1897. Paris, Verneau. 100 × 141 cm/39.5 × 55.5 in
PL.119. F. VALLOTTON	Poster for the revue "Ah! La Pe . . . La Pe . . . La Pepiniere!!!" in two acts and four tableaus. c.1895. Paris, Pajol. 129 × 93 cm/51 × 36.5 in
PL.120. FRED HYLAND	English poster for "Harper's" magazine. 1896. London, Waterlow. 75 × 50 cm/29.5 × 19.5 in
SP.PL.5. JULES CHÉRET	Original design for "Les Maîtres de l'Affiche." Collector's proof, red plus tint, without text.
SP.PL.6. T.A. STEINLEN	Original design for "Les Maîtres de l'Affiche." Collector's proof, pencil and tint, without text.
SP.PL.7. H.-G. IBELS	Original design for "Les Maîtres de l'Affiche." Collector's proof, in three colors, without text.
SP.PL.8. GEORGES DE FEURE	Original design for "Les Maîtres de l'Affiche."
PL.121. JULES CHÉRET	Poster for La Diaphane rice powder. 1890. Paris. Chaix. 124 × 88 cm/49 × 34.5 in
PL.122. TOULOUSE-LAUTREC	Poster for La Goulue's appearance at the Moulin Rouge. 1891. Paris, Ch. Lévy. 170 × 120 cm/67 × 47 in
PL.123. MAXFIELD PARRISH	American poster for "The Century" magazine. 1897. New York, Thomas & Wylie. 51 × 34 cm/20 × 13.5 in
PL.124. FRITZ REHM	German poster for Laferme cigarettes. 1897. Leipzig, Grimme & Hempel. 88 × 58 cm/34.5 × 23 in
PL.125. JULES CHÉRET	Poster for the Cadet Roussel performance at the Hippodrome featuring equestrian stunts and pantomimes every evening except Tuesdays and Fridays. 1882. Paris, Chaix. 58 × 43.5 cm/23 × 17 in
PL.126. EUGENE GRASSET	Poster for the series on Napoleon in "The Century" magazine. 1894. New York. 78 × 52 cm/30.5 × 20.5 in
PL.127. OTTO FISCHER	German poster for the Wilhelm Hoffmann's Studio for Modern Posters in Dresden. 1896. Dresden, Hoffmann. 95 × 64 cm/37.5 × 25 in
PL.128. ETHEL REED	American poster for the novel, "The Quest of the Golden Girl." 1896. London, Waterlow. 75.5 × 48.5 cm/30 × 19 in
PL.129. JULES CHÉRET	Poster for the Casino d'Enghien. (For a Charity Ball for the victims of a fire at Fort-de-France, September 21, 1890). 1890. Paris, Chaix. 124 × 88 cm/49 × 34.5 in
PL.130. GEORGES DE FEURE	Poster for the variety store, A Jeanne d'Arc, in Carcassonne. 1896. Paris, Bourgerie. 243 × 93 cm/95.5 × 36.5 in
PL.131. ALEX. CHARPENTIER	Poster for the Grande Tuilerie d'Ivry, founded in 1854. It is "the largest factory in the world for ceramic products for the construction industry and art works . . . Architectural ornaments; Decorative sculpture." 1897. Paris, Chaix. 124 × 88 cm/49 × 34.5 in
PL.132. WM. CARQUEVILLE	American poster for "Lippincott's" magazine. 1895. Philadelphia. 48 × 31 cm/19 × 12 in

PL.133. JULES CHÉRET	Poster for the Olympia. 1892. Paris, Chaix. 124 × 88 cm/49 × 34.5 in
PL.134. T.A. STEINLEN	Poster for François Coppée's novel, "Le Coupable" published in the newspaper "Le Journal" 1896. Paris, Verneau. 160 × 100 cm/63 × 39.5 in
PL.135. LUCIEN LEFÈVRE	Poster for Absinthe Mugnier, produced by Frédéric Mugnier and sold everywhere. 1895. Paris, Chaix. 245 × 88 cm/96.5 × 34.5 in
PL.136. WILL BRADLEY	American poster for "The Chap-Book." 1895. Chicago. 54 × 36 cm/ 21 × 14 in
PL.137. JULES CHÉRET	Poster for the benefit of the Emergency Night Shelters; announcing an exhibition of French Art from the period of Louis XIV and Louis XV at the Ecole des Beaux-Arts. 1888. Paris, Chaix. 124 × 88 cm/49 × 34.5 in
PL.138. H.-G. IBELS	Poster for the Exhibition of H.-G. Ibels at the Bodinière. 1894. Paris, Verneau. 65 × 50 cm/25.5 × 19.5 in
PL.139. LUCE	Poster for the performance of Mévisto at the Scala. 1891. Paris, Bataille. 179 × 67 cm/70.5 × 26.5 in
PL.140. MAURICE DENIS	Poster for the newspaper "La Dépêche" of Toulouse. "Free distribution of the April 16 and 17 issues." 1892. Paris, Ancourt. 148 × 98 cm/58 × 38.5 in
PL.141. JULES CHÉRET	Poster for the toy and gift shop, Aux Buttes Chaumont. 1887. Paris, Chaix. 267 × 108 cm/105 × 42.5 in
PL.142. WILLETTE	Poster for the International Fair of Commercial and Industrial Products on the Champ de Mars, from April 25 to August 5, 1893. 1893. Paris, Verneau. 140 × 100 cm/55 × 39.5 in
PL.143. MANUEL ROBBE	Poster for the kerosene lamp, L'Eclatante. 1895. Paris, Bourgerie. 130 × 94 cm/51 × 37 in
PL.144. ALPHONSE MUCHA	Poster for Sarah Bernhardt's appearance in the Dumas play, "La Dame aux Camélias" at the Théâtre de la Renaissance. 1896. Paris, Champenois. 207 × 77 cm/81.5 × 30.5 in

1899

PL.145. JULES CHÉRET	Poster for La Saxoleine, "a safety kerosene, extra-white, deodorized, non-flammable, dispensed in 5 liter sealed cans." 1892. Paris, Chaix. 124 × 88 cm/49 × 34.5 in
PL.146. GEORGES DE FEURE	Poster for the "Journal des Ventes" (Auction News) published in Brussels by Charles Vos. 1897. Paris, Lemercier. 65 × 50 cm/25.5 × 20 in
PL.147. GEORGES MEUNIER	Poster for the Bal Bullier. "Great celebration every Thursday, dancing on Saturdays and Sundays." 1894. Paris, Chaix. 124 × 88 cm/49 × 34.5 in
PL.148. DUDLEY HARDY	English poster for "The J.P." at London's Strand Theatre. 1898. London, Waterlow. 75 × 49 cm/29.5 × 19.5 in
PL.149. JULES CHÉRET	Poster for the Bals de l'Opéra at the Théâtre de l'Opéra January 7, 1899. 1898. Paris, Chaix. 124 × 88 cm/49 × 34.5 in
PL.150. LOUIS ANQUETIN	Poster for Marguerite Dufay. c.1894. Paris, Ancourt. 94 × 128 cm/ 37 × 50.5 in
PL.151. LÉOPOLD STEVENS	Poster for Eugénie Buffet, "the popular songstress," appearing at the Théâtre de la Republique. c.1895. Paris, Dupont. 115 × 68 cm/ 45 × 27 in

PL.152. WILL BRADLEY — American poster for Victor Bicycles. 1896. Boston, Forbes. 68 × 104 cm/27 × 41 in

PL.153. JULES CHÉRET — Poster for L'Eau de Sirènes, "a prize-winning hair dye, on sale in every beauty salon." 1888. Paris, Chaix. 157 × 115 cm/62 × 45 in

PL.154. FERNEL (F. CERCKEL) — Poster for Bonne Cafetière brand of chicory. 1898. Paris, Lemercier. 157 × 115 cm/62 × 45 in

PL.155. CHARLES LUCAS — Poster announcing the publication of Emile Zola's novel, "Rome" in "Le Journal." c.1894. Paris, Dupont. 260 × 137 cm/102 × 54 in

PL.156. HENRI MEUNIER — Belgian poster for Rajah coffee. 1897. Brussels, Goossens. 56 × 71 cm/22 × 28 in

PL.157. JULES CHÉRET — Poster for the pantomime play by Rene Maizeroy titled "Le Miroir," at the Folies-Bergere. 1892. Paris, Chaix. 121 × 82 cm/47.5 × 32.5 in

PL.158. EUGÈNE GRASSET — Poster for Encre Marquet, "the best of all inks." 1892. Paris, Malherbe. 117 × 76 cm/46 × 30 in

PL.159. J.-A. GRÜN — Poster for the revue "Chauffons!" (Let's get hot!) at La Pépinière. 1898. Paris, Chaix. 123 × 85 cm/48.5 × 33.5 in

PL.160. HOHENSTEIN — Italian poster commemorating the centennial of the discovery of the electric battery by Volta. 1898. Milan, Ricordi. 107 × 53 cm/42 × 21 in

PL.161 JULES CHÉRET — Poster for a Charity Ball at the Trocadero for the benefit of the families of shipwrecked sailors, held May 27, 1893. 1893. Paris, Chaix. 247 × 80 cm/97 × 31.5 in

PL.162. MOREAU-NÉLATON — Poster for the National Exhibition of Ceramics and all fine arts, held from May 15 to July 31, 1897, at the Palais des Beaux-Arts. 1897. Paris, Verneau. 134 × 95 cm/53 × 37.5 in

PL.163. A. GUILLAUME — Poster for Armour & Co. meat extract, "the only one that retains the flavor of fresh meat, superior to all others." 1891. Paris, Camis. 123 × 90 cm/48.5 × 35.5 in

PL.164. R. WITZEL — German poster for the illustrated monthly magazine, "Deutsche Kunst und Dekoration" (German Art and Decoration). 1898. Darmstadt, Koch. 58 × 79 cm/23 × 31 in

SP.PL.9. JULES CHÉRET — Original design for "Les Maîtres de l'Affiche." Collector's proof, red and tint, without text.

SP.PL.10. T.A. STEINLEN — Original design for "Les Maîtres de l'Affiche." Collector's proof, pencil and tint, without text.

SP.PL.11. WILLETTE — "La Pieuse Erreur" (The Pious Mistake). Original drawing for "Les Maîtres de l'Affiche." Collector's proof, in pencil, without text.

SP.PL.12. CRAFTY — Original design for "Les Maîtres de l'Affiche." Collector's proof, in pencil, without text.

PL.165. JULES CHÉRET — Poster for the Concert des Ambassadeurs. Featuring "Songs-Operettas-Ballets-Acrobats-Prestidigitation." 1884. Paris, Chaix. 115 × 80 cm/45 × 31.5 in

PL.166. ALPHONSE MUCHA — Poster for Sarah Bernhardt's appearance in Rostand's play, "La Samaritaine" at the Theatre de la Renaissance. 1897. Paris, Champenois. 169 × 54 cm/66.5 × 21 in

PL.167. GEORGES MEUNIER — Poster for Job cigarette paper. 1894. Paris, Chaix. 234 × 82 cm/92 × 32.5 in

PL.168. BEGGARSTAFF	English poster for Rowntree's Elect Cocoa. 1895. 95 × 70 cm/37.5 × 27.5 in
PL.169. JULES CHÉRET	Poster for the toy and gift shop, Aux Buttes Chaumont. 1889. Paris, Chaix. 267 × 108 cm/105 × 42.5 in
PL.170. T.A. STEINLEN	Poster for the French Chocolate and Tea Co. 1896. Paris, Courmont. 76 × 55 cm/30 × 21.5 in
PL.171. F. HUGO D'ALÉSI	Poster for the Eastern Railroad Co. "From Paris to Venice via Belfort, Basel, Lucern and St. Gothard." c.1890. Paris, Courmont. 102 × 62 cm/40 × 24.5 in
PL.172. WILL BRADLEY	American poster for the Christmas 1895 issue of "The Inland Printer." 1895. 44 × 36 cm/17.5 × 14 in
PL.173. JULES CHÉRET	Poster for the P.L.M. Railroad company's service to Auvergne. "Trains from Paris to Vichy, Clermont-Ferrand and Châtel-Guyon . . . Detailed prospectus available in the network's major stations." 1892. Paris, Chaix. 98 × 70 cm/38.5 × 27.5 in
PL.174. EUGÈNE GRASSET	Poster for Sarah Bernhardt's appearance in "Jeanne d'Arc" at the Theatre de la Renaissance. 1893. Paris, Malherbe. 114 × 70 cm/45 × 27.5 in
PL.175. PAUL BERTHON	Poster for Violin and music lessons. 1898. Paris, Chaix. 40 × 54 cm/16 × 21 in
PL.176. VACLAVOLIVA	Czech poster for the illustrated journal "Zlata Praha." Subscription is 2 florins per trimester. c.1898. Prague, Otto. 100 × 35 cm/39.5 × 14 in
PL.177. JULES CHÉRET	Poster for the Paris Hippodrome production at the Olympia, London. 1887. Paris, Chaix. 250 × 96 cm/98.5 × 38 in
PL.178. MOREAU-NÉLATON	Poster for the Pardon of Saint-Jean-du-Doigt (St. John of the Finger). Archeological curiosities. Hotel-Pension St. Jean. 1894. Paris, Verneau. 130 × 91 cm/51 × 36 in
PL.179. ROEDEL	Poster for the publication "La Vache Enragée" (The Mad Cow). 1897. Paris, Chaix. 115 × 78 cm/45.5 × 30.5 in
PL.180. HOHENSTEIN	Italian poster for the comic-opera "Iris." 1898. Milan, Ricordi. 120 × 65 cm/47 × 25.5 in
PL.181. JULES CHÉRET	Poster for the World's Fair of 1889. "The Land of the Fairies . . . The enchanted garden." 1889. Paris, Chaix. 73 × 54 cm/29 × 21 in
PL.182. ALPHONSE MUCHA	Poster for the Beers of the Meuse. 1898. Paris, Champenois. 139 × 88 cm/55 × 34.5 in
PL.183. GEORGES FAY	Poster for Amieux-Freres sardines and canned foods. "11 factories employing 3,500 workers, producing 12 million cans per year." 1899. Paris, Vercasson. 85 × 130 cm/33.5 × 51 in
PL.184. BEGGARSTAFF	English poster for "A Trip to Chinatown," a musical show by Charles H. Hoyt. 1895. London, Dangerfield. 295 × 195 cm/116 × 76.5 in
PL.185. JULES CHÉRET	Poster for the toy and gift shop, Aux Buttes Chaumont. 1888. Paris, Chaix. 254 × 98 cm/100 × 38.5 in
PL.186. J.-L. FORAIN	Poster for the Exhibition of Women's Art at the Palais de l'Industrie. "The Parisian Woman of the Century." 1892. Paris, Chaix. 162 × 114 cm/64 × 45 in
PL.187. LORANT-HEILBRONN & V. GUILLET	Poster for the opera "Messaline" at the Monte Carlo Theatre. 1898. Paris, Dupont. 200 × 73 cm/78.5 × 29 in

PL.188. RUDOLF KOLLER	Swiss poster for the Jubilee Exhibition at the Zurich Artists' House. 1898. Zurich, Poligraph Institut. 103 × 73 cm/40.5 × 29 in
PL.189. JULES CHÉRET	Poster for the Louvre Department Store. 1891. Paris, Chaix. 235 × 80 cm/90.5 × 31.5 in
PL.190. T.A. STEINLEN	Poster for Comiot motorcycles. 1899. Paris, Verneau. 133 × 92 cm/52.5 × 36 in
PL.191. RENÉ PÉAN	Poster for the Department Store, A la Place Clichy. "Novelties of the season. Distribution of bouquets from Nice." 1898. Paris, Chaix. 124 × 88 cm/49 × 34.5 in
PL.192. G. BOANO	Italian poster for Torino's Royal Theatre. (Shown here is actually the top half of a two-sheet poster; bottom had largely type, to announce the various operas performed there.) 1898. Milan, Ricordi. 121 × 84 cm/47.5 × 33 in

1900

PL.193. JULES CHÉRET	First panel, without text, titled "The Dance." 1891. Paris, Chaix. 124 × 88 cm/49 × 34.5 in
PL.194. WILLETTE	Poster for the Exhibition of Charlet's works and of modern lithographs, organized by the Society of French Lithographic Artists under the auspices of the Minister of Education. 1893. Paris, Belfond. 60 × 94 cm/23.5 × 37 in
PL.195. ROEDEL	Poster for Linge Monopole: "linen shirts and underwear specially treated, no ironing required." 1897. Paris, Chaix. 115 × 82 cm/45 × 32 in
PL.196. HENRI MEUNIER	Belgian poster for Starlight soap. 1899. Brussels, Rycker. 82 × 40 cm/32 × 16 in
PL.197. JULES CHÉRET	Second panel, without text, titled "The Music." 1891. Paris. Chaix. 124 × 88 cm/49 × 34.5 in
PL.198. MOREAU-NÉLATON	Poster for Notre Dame Cathedral. "French workers, bring your stone to Notre-Dame du Travail. Send your contributions to the Priest, 10 Schomer Street, Paris." 1897. Paris, Verneau. 128 × 93 cm/50.6 × 36.5 in
PL.199. GEORGES DE FEURE	Poster for Indian teas. c.1895. Paris, J. Weiner. 95 × 73 cm/37.5 × 29 in
PL.200. LOUIS RHEAD	American poster for "The Sun" newspaper. 1896. New York, Liebler & Maas. 118 × 73 cm/46.5 × 29 in
PL.201. JULES CHÉRET	Third panel, without text, titled "The Pantomime." 1891. Paris, Chaix. 124 × 88 cm/49 × 34.5 in
PL.202. ALPHONSE MUCHA	Poster for Job cigarette paper. 1898. Paris, Champenois. 51 × 39 cm/20 × 15.5 in
PL.203. E. BARCET	Poster for the Pompadour Theatre. c.1898. Paris, Verneau. 76 × 62 cm/30 × 24.5 in
PL.204. A. DE RIQUER	Spanish poster for Maison A. and E. Napoléon, photographers in Barcelona. 1895. (no size given).
PL.205. JULES CHÉRET	Fourth panel, without text, titled "The Comedy." 1891. Paris, Chaix. 124 × 88 cm/49 × 34.5 in
PL.206. C. LÉANDRE	Poster for the Gallery of Modern Artists' First Exhibit of the Society of Painters and Lithographers. 1897. Paris, Malfeyt. 104 × 71 cm/41 × 28 in

PL.207. FERNEL (F. CERCKEL)	Poster for the Bazar des Halles et des Postes stores. Toys and Gifts. 1899. Paris, Chaix. 118 × 84 cm/46.5 × 33 in
PL.208. ARPAD BASCH	Hungarian poster for Kuhnee company, "the oldest Hungarian company constructing agricultural machinery. Producers of the famous brands: Hungaria and Moson." 1899. Budapest, Kosmos Muintezet. 41 × 69 cm/16 × 27 in
SP.PL.13. JULES CHÉRET	Original design for "Les Maîtres de l'Affiche." Collector's proof, in three colors, without text.
SP.PL.14. PAUL BERTHON	Original design for "Les Maîtres de l'Affiche." Collector's proof, in three colors, without text.
SP.PL.15. C. LÉANDRE	Original design for "Les Maîtres de l'Affiche." Collector's proof. "Mimi Pinson has become a great lady; she will never take her coachman as her lover."
SP.PL.16. JULES CHÉRET	Original design for "Les Maîtres de l'Affiche." Collector's proof, red and tint, without text.
PL.209. JULES CHÉRET	Poster for the newspaper "Le Rappel." 1889. Paris, Chaix. 170 × 115 cm/67 × 45 in
PL.210. CHARLES LUCAS	Poster for Felicien Champsaur's "Entrance of a Female Clown." c.1897. Paris, Verneau. 188 × 60 cm/74 × 23.5 in
PL.211. RENÉ PÉAN	Poster for the Oriental Carpets store, Aux Trois Quartiers. 1899. Paris, Chaix. 150 × 100 cm/59 × 39.5 in
PL.212. PRIVAT LIVEMONT	Belgian poster for the Cercle Artistique de Schaerbeek's 5th yearly exhibition. 1897. Brussels, Trommer et Staeves. 100 × 77 cm/39.5 × 30.5 in
PL.213. JULES CHÉRET	Poster for Pippermint, produced by Get brothers and available in all cafés, groceries and wine stores. 1899. Paris, Chaix. 105 × 81 cm/41.5 × 32 in
PL.214. ORAZI & GORGUET	Poster for the play "Théodora" at the Theatre de la Porte Saint-Martin. 1884. Paris, Delanchy. 129 × 93 cm/51 × 36.5 in
PL.215. MISTI	Poster for the newspaper "La Critique." 1896. Paris, Verneau. 53 × 33 cm/21 × 13 in
PL.216. DUDLEY HARDY	English poster for the weekly magazine, "To-Day." c.1895. London, David Allen. 295 × 195 cm/116 × 76.5 in
PL.217. JULES CHÉRET	Poster for the Taverne Olympia, a restaurant open all night and featuring a Ladies' orchestra as well as roller coasters. 1899. Paris, Chaix. 118 × 81 cm/46.5 × 32 in
PL.218. G. FRAIPONT	Poster for the Northern Railroad Company, announcing excursions to Pierrefonds, Compiègne and Coucy-le-Château. c.1897. Paris, Fraipont & Moreau. 98 × 70 cm/38.5 × 27.5 in
PL.219. F. GOTTLOB	Poster for the Second Exhibition of Painters and Lithographers at the Salle du Figaro. 1899. Paris, Lemercier. 112 × 74 cm/44 × 29 in
PL.220. LOUIS RHEAD	American poster for the newspaper "Morning Journal." 1895. New York, Liebler & Mass. 45 × 115 cm/17.5 × 45 in
PL.221. JULES CHÉRET	Poster for the Grand Theatre de l'Exposition. The Children's Palace. 1889. Paris, Chaix. 240 × 90 cm/94.5 × 35.5 in
PL.222. H. THOMAS	Poster for the politically independent newspaper, "L'Eclair." (Winner of First Prize in the poster contest sponsored by "L'Eclair.") 1897. Paris, Chaix. 125 × 90 cm/49 × 35.5 in

PL.223. J.-A. GRÜN — Poster for the Railway of the West and the London, Brighton and South Coast Railway. "The Compagnie de L'Ouest will send you free of charge a guidebook of London . . . Paris to London. Fast Service, day and night from the St. Lazare Station." 1899. Paris, Chaix. 100 × 70 cm/39.5 × 27.5 in

PL.224. A. RASSENFOSSE — Belgian poster for a wrestling contest from Liège at La Fontaine. 1899. Liège, Bénard. 100 × 74 cm/39.5 × 29 in

PL.225. JULES CHÉRET — Poster for the book "La Gomme" (Phony Dealings) by Félicien Champsaur. 1889. Paris, Chaix. 88 × 120 cm/34.5 × 47 in

PL.226. RÉALIER-DUMAS — Poster for the 15th Exhibition of the International Society of Painters and Sculptors held at the Galerie Georges Petit. (The posterist is one of the featured artists). 1897. Paris, Verneau. 130 × 94 cm/51 × 37 in

PL.227. PAUL BERTHON — Poster for the illustrated magazine, "L'Ermitage." 1897. Étampes, Énard. 62 × 44 cm/24.5 × 17.5 in

PL.228. H. CASSIERS — Belgian poster for the Red Star Line, Antwerp to New York. 1899. Brussels, Rycker & Mendel. 86 × 58 cm/34 × 23 in

PL.229. JULES CHÉRET — Poster for the production "La Marche au Soleil" (The March into the Sun) at La Bodinière. 1900. Paris, Chaix. 125 × 89 cm/49 × 35 in

PL.230. ROCHEGROSSE — Poster for the musical "Louise" at the Théâtre National de l'Opéra Comique. 1900. Paris, Delanchy. 80 × 60 cm/31.5 × 23.5 in.

PL.231. GEORGES FAY — Poster for the Central Syndicat of French Farmers. 1900. Paris, Vercasson. 110 × 150 cm/43.5 × 59 in

PL.232. BEGGARSTAFF — English poster for Kassama corn flour. 1894. London, Henderson. 143 × 95 cm/56.5 × 37.5 in

PL.233. JULES CHÉRET — Poster for L'Auréole du Midi, a "safety kerosene, extra white and odorless. Comes in 5 liter sealed canisters." 1893. Paris, Chaix. 122 × 88 cm/48 × 34.5 in

PL.234. CHARLES LUCAS — Poster for the Cabaret des Arts. 1896. Paris, Chaix. 126 × 90 cm/49.5 × 35.5 in

PL.235. ROEDEL — Poster for the Salon National de la Mode "under the auspices of the fashion department of the 'Petit Journal' at the Palais des Beaux Arts." Customer is holding "Beauty Tips of Lenthéric." c.1898. Paris, Chardin. 218 × 112 cm/86 × 44 in

PL.236. REISNER — Czech poster for a jewelry store, F & D Maly, in Prague. c.1898. Prague, Vitek. 95 × 63 cm/37.5 × 25 in

PL.237. JULES CHÉRET — Poster for the Palais de Glace (Ice Palace) at the Champs Elysées. 1893. Paris, Chaix. 236 × 82 cm/93 × 32.5 in

PL.238. TOULOUSE-LAUTREC — Poster for La Chaine Simpson (the bicycle chain by Simpson) sold in France by L.B. Spoke. 1896. Paris, Chaix. 80 × 118 cm/31.5 × 46.5 in

PL.239. F. GOTTLOB — Poster for Gottlob's exhibition at Salon des Cent. 1898. Paris, Chaix. 55 × 36 cm/21.5 × 14 in

PL.240. VAN CASPEL — Dutch poster for the Whoogenstraten company, purveyors of fine vegetables, soups and sauces. c.1898. Rotterdam, Senefelder. 70 × 47 cm/27.5 × 18.5 in

ALPHABETICAL TABLE OF ARTISTS' NAMES

LOUIS ANQUETIN
Marguerite Dufay, pl. 150.
FERDINAND BAC
Yvette Guilbert (Scala), pl. 19.
E. BARCET
Théâtre Pompadour, pl. 203.
ARPAD BASCH
Maison Kühnee (Machines agricoles), pl. 208.
BEGGARSTAFF
Harper's Magazine, pl. 16.
Don Quixote, pl. 63.
Hamlet, pl. 107.
Rowntree's Elect Cocoa, pl. 168.
A Trip to Chinatown, pl. 184.
Corn Flour Kassama, pl. 232.
EMILE BERCHMANS
Salon de 1896, à Liège, pl. 108.
PAUL BERTHON
Leçons de Violon, pl. 175.
Original design for *Maitres de l'Affiche.* Sp.Pl.14.
Revue "L'Ermitage", pl. 227.
G. BOANO
Théâtre royal de Turin, pl. 192.
PIERRE BONNARD
La Revue Blanche, pl. 38.
FIRMIN BOUISSET
Chocolat Menier, pl. 47.
BOUTET DE MONVEL
Pâte dentifrice du docteur Pierre, pl. 26.
La Petite Poucette, pl. 106.
WILL. BRADLEY
When hearts are trumps, pl. 52.
The Chap-Book, pl. 136.
Victor Bicycles, pl. 152.
Inland Printer, pl. 172.
CARAN D'ACHE
Exposition russe, pl. 70.
WM. CARQUEVILLE
Lippincott's Magazine, pl. 44.
Lippincott's Magazine, pl. 132.
H. CASSIERS
Red Star Line, pl. 228.
CAZALS
7e Exposition du Salon des Cent, pl. 15.
ALEX. CHARPENTIER
Grande Tuilerie d'Ivry, pl. 131.
JULES CHÉRET
Papier á cigarettes Job, pl. 1.
Punch Grassot, pl. 5.
Grand Veglione de Gala, à l'Opéra, pl. 9.
La Saxoléine, pl. 13.
Le Palais de Glace, pl. 17.
L'Arc-en-ciel, pl. 21.
Lidia, pl. 25.
Quinquina Dubonnet, pl. 29.
Le Théâtrophone, pl. 33.
Les Coulisses de l'Opéra, pl. 37.
Pantomimes lumineuses, pl. 41.
L'Amant des Danseuses, pl. 45.
Original design for "Les Maîtres de l'Affiche," Sp.Pl. 1, 2, 3, 5, 9, 13, 16.
Le Courrier Français, pl. 49.
Bal du Moulin Rouge, pl. 53.
Bal masqué de l'Opéra 1897, pl. 57.
Paris-Courses, pl. 61.
Jardin de Paris, pl. 65.
La Terre, pl. 69.
La Loïe Fuller, pl. 73.
Vin Mariani, pl. 77.
Pan, pl. 81.
Redoute des Étudiants, pl. 85.
Fête de charité au bénéfice de la Société de Secours aux Familles des Marins naufragés, pl. 89.
Camille Stefani, pl. 93.
Exposition de Tableaux et Dessins de A. Willette, pl. 97.
Fête des Fleurs de Bagnères-de-Luchon, pl. 101.
2e Bal de l'Opéra, 5 février 1898, pl. 105.
Quinquina Dubonnet, pl. 109.
Émilienne d'Alençon, pl. 113.
Œuvres de Rabelais, pl. 117.
La Diaphane, pl. 121.
Cadet Roussel, pl. 125.
Casino d'Enghien, pl. 129.
Olympia, pl. 133.
Œuvre de l'Hospitalité de Nuit, pl. 137.
Aux Buttes-Chaumont, pl. 141.
Saxoléine, pl. 145.
Bals de l'Opéra en 1899, pl. 149.
Eau des Sirènes, pl. 153.
Le Miroir, 157.
Fête de Charité, pl. 161.
Concert des Ambassadeurs, pl. 165.
Aux Buttes-Chaumont (1889). pl. 169.
L'Auvergne, pl. 173.
Exhibition d'Arabes du Sahara, pl. 177.
Le Pays des Fées, pl. 181.
Aux Buttes-Chaumont, (1888), pl. 185.
Magasins du Louvre, pl. 189.
First panel: la Danse, pl. 193.
Second panel: la Musique, pl. 197.
Third panel: la Pantomime, pl. 201.
Fourth panel: la Comédie, pl. 205.
Journal "le Rappel", pl. 209.
Pippermint, pl. 213.
Taverne Olympia, pl. 217.
Grand Théâtre de l'Exposition (1889), pl. 221.
La Gomme, pl. 225.
La Bodinière, pl. 229.
L'Auréole du Midi. pl. 233.
Palais de Glace, pl. 237.
CRAFTY
Original design for "Les Maîtres de l'Affiche," Sp.Pl.12.
A. CRESPIN
Paul Hankar, architect, pl. 91.
MAURICE DENIS
La Dépêche de Toulouse, pl. 140.
AUGUSTE DONNAY
Concours international de chant, à Liège, pl. 59.
ARTHUR W. DOW
Modern Art, pl. 36.
ED. DUYCK & A. CRESPIN
Ferme de Frahinfaz, pl. 28.
HYLAND ELLIS
The Gay Parisienne, pl. 96.
H. EVENEPOËL
Anvers et son Exposition, pl. 116.
GEORGES FAY
Sardines Amieux, pl. 183.
Syndicat central des Agriculteurs de France, pl. 231.
FERNEL (F. CERCKEL)
Chicorée Bonne Cafetière, pl. 154.
Bazar des Halles et Postes, pl. 207.
GEORGES DE FEURE
5e Exposition du Salon des Cent, pl. 10.
Original design for "Les Maîtres de l'Affiche," Sp.Pl.8.
A Jeanne d'Arc, pl. 130.
Le Journal des Ventes, pl. 146.
Thés du Palais Indien, pl. 199.
OTTO FISCHER
Ausstellung, Dresden, 1896, pl. 68.
Kunst-Anstalt fur Moderne Plakate, pl. 127.
PAUL FISCHER
Exhibition of Wilh. Söborg, pl. 84.
J.-L. FORAIN
Salon du Cycle, pl. 51.
La Parisienne du Siècle, pl. 186.
G. FRAIPONT
Pierrefonds, pl. 218.
LÉO GAUSSON
Lessive Figaro, pl. 71.
H. GERBAULT
Chocolat Carpentier, pl. 83.
ALICE R. GLENNY
Women's edition, Buffalo Courier, pl. 60.
GORGUET & ORAZI
Théodora, pl. 214.
F. GOTTLOB
Deuxième Exposition des Peintres-Lithographes, pl. 219.
Salon des Cent, pl. 239.
EUGÈNE GRASSET
A la Place Clichy, pl. 18.
Librairie Romantique, pl. 42.
Fêtes de Paris, pl. 50.
Exposition E. Grasset, pl. 98.
Napoléon, pl. 126.
Encre Marquet, pl. 158.
Jeanne d'Arc, pl. 174.
M. GREIFFENHAGEN
Pall Mall Budget, pl. 24.
J.-A. GRÜN
Café Riche, pl. 103.
Chauffons! Chauffons! pl. 159.
Paris-Londres, pl. 223.
A. GUILLAUME
Gigolette, pl. 30.
Extrait de Viande Armour, pl. 163.
V. GUILLET & LORANT-HEILBRONN
Messaline, pl. 187.
DUDLEY HARDY
A Gaiety Girl, pl. 4.
The Chieftain, pl. 48.
Abbotts Phit-Eesi, pl. 92.
"The J. P.," Strand Theatre, pl. 148.
To Day, pl. 216.
FRANK HAZENPLUG
Living Posters, pl. 87.

HOHENSTEIN
Centenaire de la Découverte de la Pile voltaïque, pl. 160.
Opéra-Comique "Iris", pl. 180.

F. HUGO D'ALÉSI
Centenaire de la Lithographie, pl. 66.
Venise, pl. 171.

FRED HYLAND
Harper's Magazine, pl. 120.

HYNAÏS
Exposition Ethnographique de Prague, pl. 56.

H.-G. IBELS
L'Escarmouche, pl. 6.
Mévisto, pl. 78.
Affiches artistiques Pierrefort, pl. 102.
Original design for "Les Maîtres de l'Affiche," Sp.Pl.7.
Exposition de H.-G. Ibels, pl. 138.

RUDOLF KOLLER
Jubilaüms Ausstellung, pl. 188.

TOULOUSE-LAUTREC
Divan Japonais, pl. 2.
La Revue Blanche, pl. 82.
Jane Avril, pl. 110.
La Goulue, pl. 122.
Chaîne Simpson, pl. 238.

C. LÉANDRE
Galerie des Artistes modernes, pl. 206.
Original design for "Les Maîtres de l'Affiche," Sp.Pl.15.

LUCIEN LEFÈVRE
Cacao lacté, pl. 11.
L'Électricine, pl. 55.
Cirage Jacquot, pl. 90.
Absinthe Mugnier, pl. 135.

LORANT-HEILBRONN & V. GUILLET
Messaline, Pl. 187.

CHARLES LUCAS
Rome, pl. 155.
Entrée de Clownesse, pl. 210.
Cabaret des Arts, pl. 234.

LUCE
Mévisto, pl. 139.

G. MATALONI
Incandescenza a Gas, pl. 72.

GEORGES MEUNIER
Frossard's Cavour Cigars, pl. 7.
Excursions en Normandie et en Bretagne, pl. 31.
Trianon Concert, pl. 62.
Bal Bullier, pl. 147.
Papier à Cigarettes Job, pl. 167.

LUCIEN MÉTIVET
Eugénie Buffet (Ambassadeurs), pl. 22.

HENRI MEUNIER
Concerts Ysaye, pl. 40.
Café Rajah, pl. 156.
Savon Starlight, pl. 196.

MISTI
Cycles Gladiator, pl. 86.
Journal "la Critique", pl. 215.

MOREAU-NÉLATON
2e Exposition des Arts de la Femme, pl. 58.
La Nativité, pl. 118.
Exposition nationale de la Céramique, pl. 162.
Pardon de Saint-Jean-du-Doigt, pl. 178.
Notre-Dame-du-Travail, pl. 198.

A. G. MORROW
The New Woman, pl. 79.

ALPHONSE MUCHA
Gismonda, pl. 27.
20e Exposition du Salon des Cent, pl. 94.
Lorenzaccio, pl. 114.
La Dame aux Camélias, pl. 144.
La Samaritaine, pl. 166.
Bières de la Meuse, pl. 182.
Papier à Cigarettes Job, pl. 202.

GASTON NOURY
Pour les Pauvres de France et de Russie, pl. 39.

VACLAV OLIVA
Topic Salon, pl. 100.
Zlata Praha, pl. 176

ORAZI & GORGUET
Théodora, pl. 214.

PAL
Grand ballet Brighton, pl. 35.

MAXFIELD PARRISH
The Century Magazine, pl. 123.

EDWARD PENFIELD
Harper's Magazine, pl. 20.
Harper's Magazine, pl. 115.

RENÉ PÉAN
A la Place Clichy, pl. 191.
Aux Trois Quartiers, pl. 211.

JULIUS PRICE
An Artist's Model, pl. 3.

PRIVAT-LIVEMONT
Casino de Cabourg, pl. 88.
Absinthe Robette, pl. 104.
Cercle artistique de Schaerbeek, pl. 212.

PUVIS DE CHAVANNES
L'Enfance de Sainte Geneviève, pl. 54.

ARMAND RASSENFOSSE
Grande Brasserie Van Velsen, pl. 12.
Tournoi de lutte, pl. 224.

M. RÉALIER-DUMAS
L'Incandescence par le Gaz, pl. 23.
Champagne Jules Mumm, pl. 111.
Galerie Georges Petit, pl. 226.

ETHEL REED
Miss Traumereï, pl. 99.
Quest of the Golden Girl, pl. 128.

FRITZ REHM
Cigaretten Laferme, pl. 124.

REISNER
F. & D. Maly, pl. 236.

LOUIS RHEAD
The Sun, pl. 8.
The Sun, pl. 200.
Morning Journal, pl. 220.

A. DE RIQUER
3ra Exposicion de Bella Artes, pl. 64.
A. & E. Napoleon Fotografos, pl. 204.

MANUEL ROBBE
L'Eclatante, pl. 143.

ROCHEGROSSE
Louise, pl. 230.

RŒDEL
Moulin de la Galette, pl. 75.
La Vache enragée, pl. 179.
Linge Monopole, pl. 195.
Salon de la Mode, pl. 235.

JOSEPH SATTLER
Pan, pl. 67.

CARLOZ SCHWABE
Salon de la Rose + Croix, pl. 74.

T. A. STEINLEN
Hellé, pl. 34.
Mothu et Doria, pl. 46.
Lait pur stérilisé de la Vingeanne, pl. 95.
Original design for "Les Maîtres de l'Affiche," Sp. Pl. 6.
Le Coupable, pl. 134.
Original design for "Les Maîtres de l'Affiche," Sp. Pl. 10.
Chocolat de la Compagnie Française, pl. 170.
Motocycles Comiot, pl. 190.

LÉOPOLD STEVENS
Eugénie Buffet, pl. 151.

M. L. STOWELL
George Humphrey's Bookstore, pl. 76.

H. THOMAS
Journal "l'Éclair", pl. 222.

FERNAND TOUSSAINT
Le Sillon, pl. 80.

F. VALLOTTON
Ah! la Pé . . . la Pé . . . la Pépinière, pl. 119.

VAN CASPEL
Whoogenstraaten et Co., pl. 240.

WILLETTE
L'Enfant prodigue, pl. 14.
Cacao Van Houten, pl. 43.
Original design for "Les Maîtres de l'Affiche," Sp. Pl. 4.
Exposition internationale des Produits du Commerce et de l'Industrie, pl. 142.
Original design for "Les Maîtres de L'Affiche," Sp. Pl. 11.
Exposition Charlet, pl. 194.

R. WITZEL
Deutsche Kunst und Dekoration, pl. 164.

CHARLES H. WOODBURY
The Century Magazine, pl. 32.
Society of Painters in Watercolor of Holland, pl. 112.

PL. 4

PL. 7

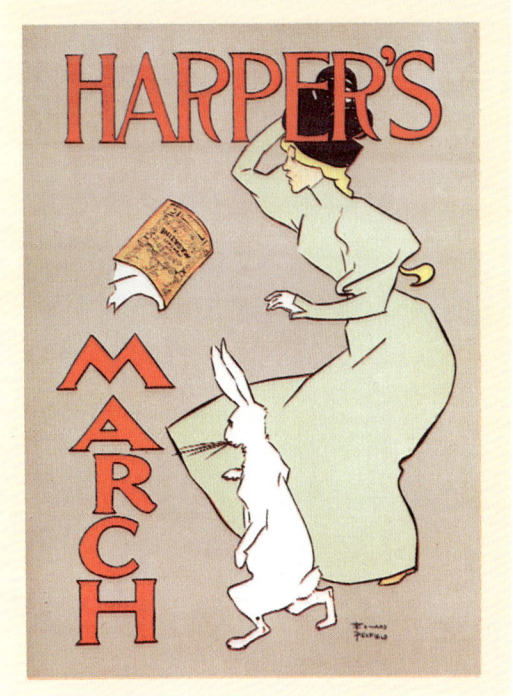

PL. 1

SP. PL. 2

PL. 3

SP. PL. 4

1897

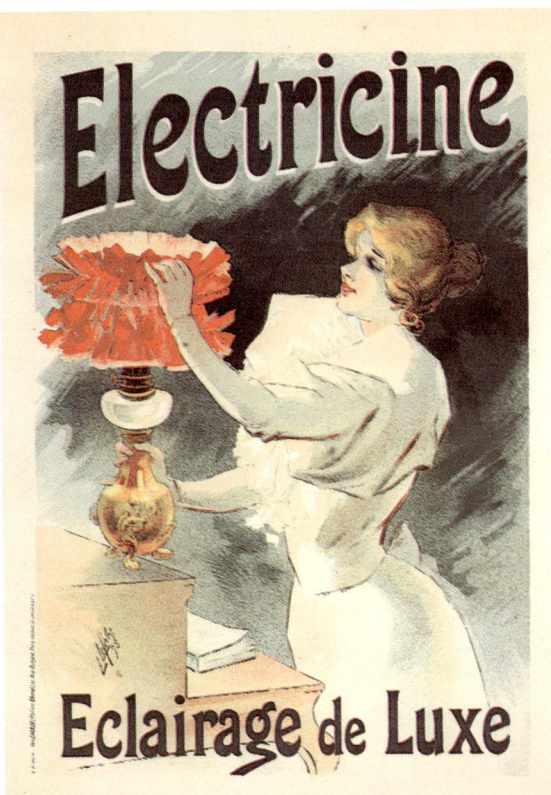

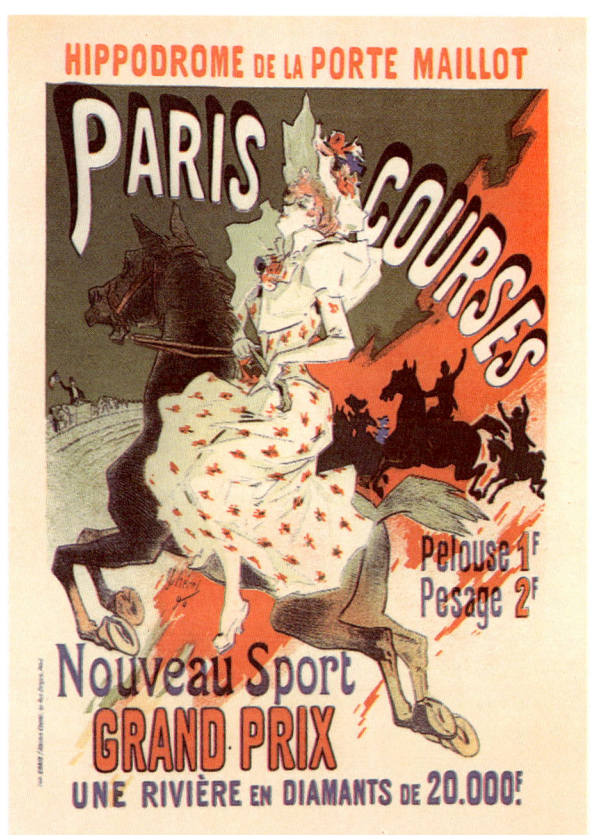

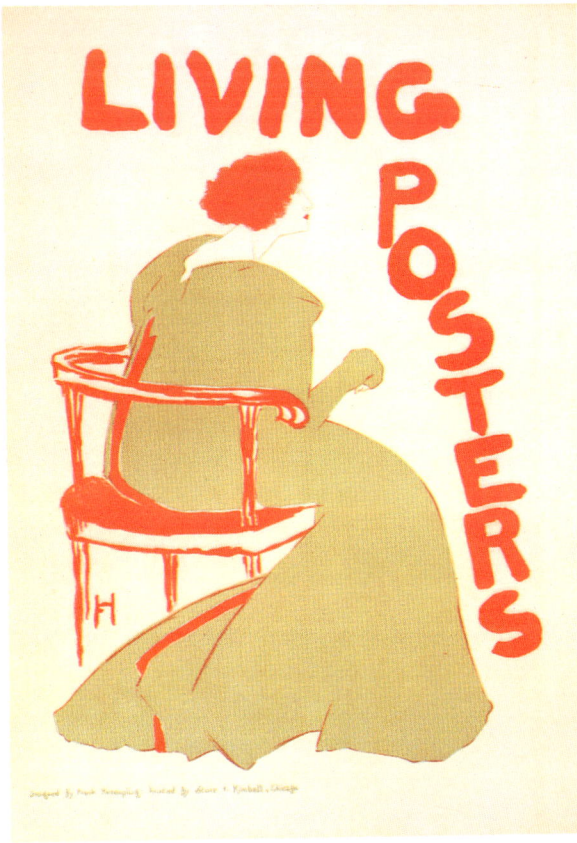

1898

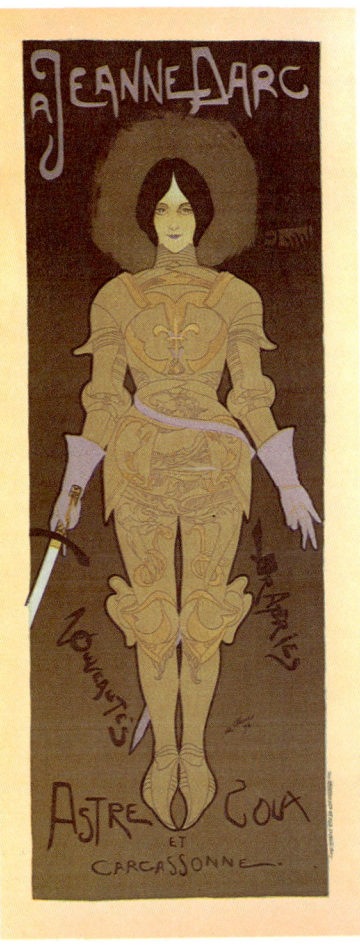

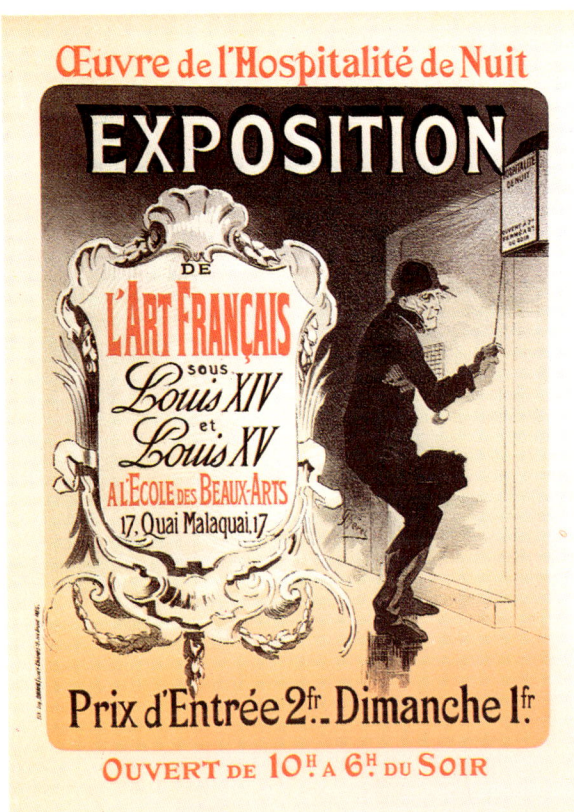

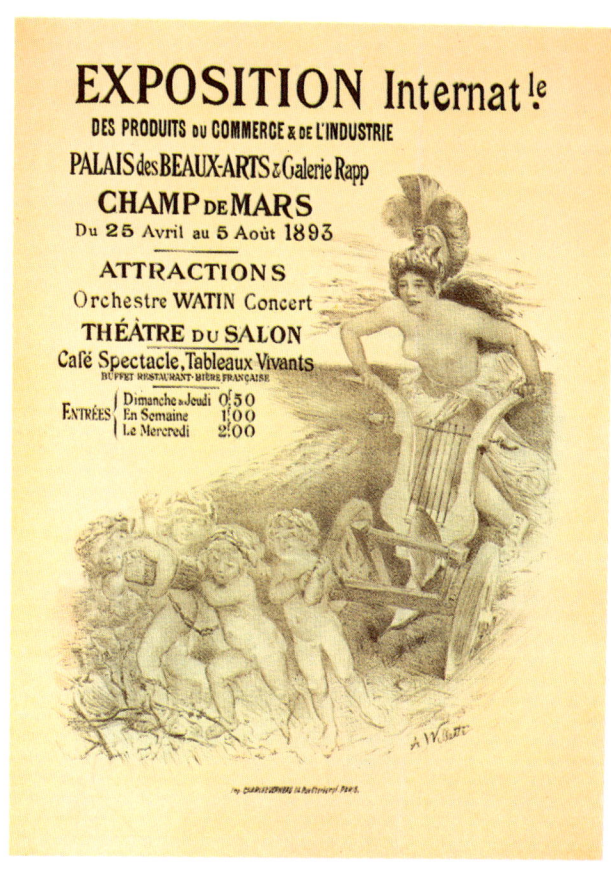

1899

PL. 154

PL. 156

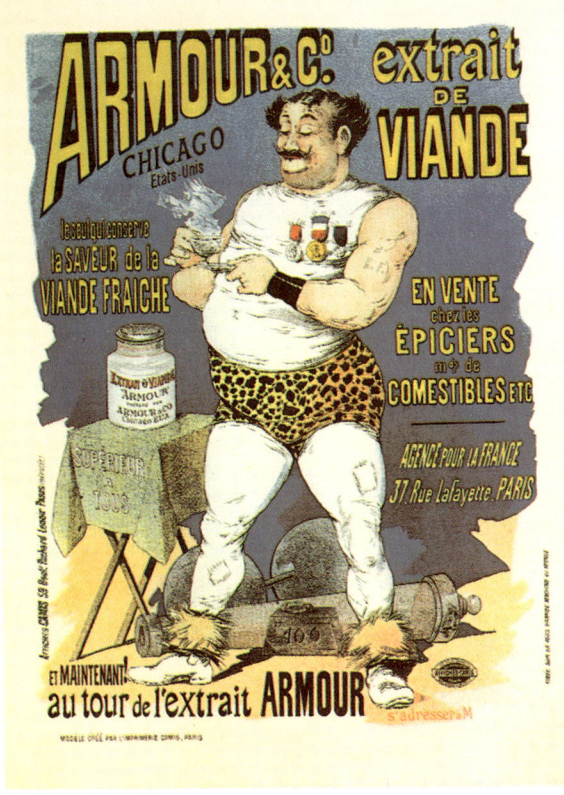

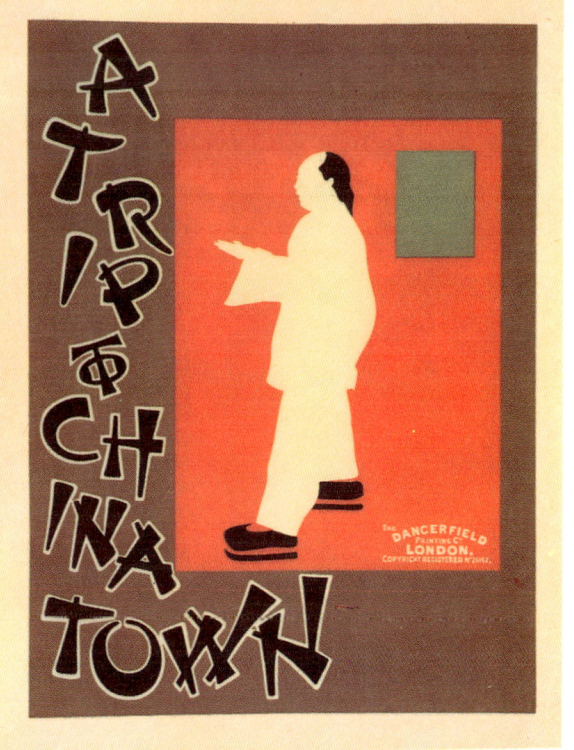

1900

PL. 198

PL. 200

PL. 221

PL. 223